Books by Richard Lederer

The Miracle of Language
The Play of Words
Crazy English
Get Thee To a Punnery
Anguished English
Basic Verbal Skills (with Philip Burnham)

····THE····
Miracle
····of····
LANGUAGE

RICHARD LEDERER

POCKET BOOKS

New York   London   Toronto   Sydney   Tokyo   Singapore

POCKET BOOKS, a division of Simon & Schuster Inc.
1230 Avenue of the Americas, New York, NY 10020

*To my father and my mother
and my sisters and my brothers*

ACKNOWLEDGMENTS

Thanks to Anne Lederer, my daughter, for making "How Do We Know What We Know?" a family affair; to Marty Capodice for the research on "One Word Can Change the World"; to Marlene Archer for suggesting so many brave new words; to Andre Hurtgen for his wisdom about foreign languages; to Beverly McDonald, Gertrude King Ramstrom, Lorraine Stickney, and Larry Katzenbach for their compact and indestructible contributions to this book; and to my students at St. Paul's School, especially Charles Shaffer, Celia Wren, Jennifer Horne, and Ashley Elinor, for their enrichment of these chapters.

I am especially grateful to my editor Jane Rosenman, whose work so embodies an abiding love for the miracle of language.

Versions of some of the chapters in this book have appeared in *Verbatim*, *Writer's Digest*, and *Writing!*

CONTENTS

Introduction   *xiii*

⋙ I ⋘

WINGED WORDS

The Miracle of Language   *3*
How Do We Know What We Know?   *11*
In Praise of English   *19*
The Case for Short Words   *33*
English at Play   *38*
Brave New Words of the 1980s   *44*

⟫⟫ II ⟪⟪

CRACKS IN THE PANE

Is English Prejudiced?   *51*
Words We Need   *62*
The Department of Redundancy
   Department   *72*
One Word Can Change the World   *79*

⟫⟫ III ⟪⟪

THE LOOM OF LITERATURE

Literary Wordmakers   *87*
A Man of Fire-New Words   *92*
No Harmless Drudges, They   *102*
The Word Magic of Lewis Carroll   *115*
The Year of Mark Twain   *123*
The Hilltop of the Heart   *134*

The Legacy of T. S. Eliot   *141*
George Orwell Is Watching You   *146*

⋙ IV ⋘

WRITE ON!

Bookmobility   *159*
A Celebration of Libraries   *168*
Ya Got Any Good Books Here?   *173*
What Is Poetry?   *177*
You Can Be a Poet   *182*
A Letter Is Forever   *193*

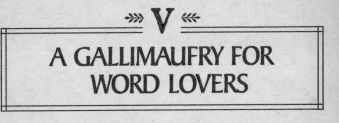

⋙ V ⋘

A GALLIMAUFRY FOR WORD LOVERS

Words About Words   *205*

Index   *245*

INTRODUCTION

A few years ago my daughter Katy was getting ready to play in a jazz band concert at our local junior high school. Her group was scheduled to perform after the orchestra and the regular band, and I, not wanting to hear other people's unidentifiable children extracting unidentifiable sounds from unidentifiable instruments—and not knowing my brass from my oboe anyway—asked some other parents to take Katy to the concert, where I would come to see her at the appropriate time.

Just as I was about to leave for the performance, the telephone rang. One of my New Hampshire Public Radio listeners wanted to know, "Why is it *sheep* and *cattle* on the hoof but *mutton* and *beef* on the table?" I get calls like this all the time, just as each day in my mailbox piles of letters about language greet me from readers of my weekly newspaper column, "Looking at Language." From the citizens of Concord, New Hampshire, alone, a megalopolis of some 35,000 souls, I have received more than enough inquiries and observations about word and phrase origins, bloopers, puns, grammar, usage, and spelling to fill my column space in the *Concord Monitor* at least once a month for the past ten years. My adventures in columny and radio commentary have led to a career as an itinerant lecturer. Many a night have I traveled to a small New England library, school, or city hall to speak to and with a group of townspeople who have come through the darkness to spend an evening in a clean, well-lighted place rapping about language.

That's one of the strange paradoxes about our times. The standard Sunday supplement jeremiads tell us of the decline of language, how the seductive luminescence of film and television and the hum and buzz of video games are blinding and deafening us to the meanings and nuances of words. But whatever you may be hearing about the closing of the American mind and cultural illiteracy (I do not deny that much of it is true), there has never been a more passionate moment in the history of the American love affair with language. Visit your local bookstore and count the volumes that line the shelves of the Language, Humor, and Reference sections; look in your local newspaper, and you may well find a column about language by somebody like me.

It is the best of times to be a person who makes his or her living spreading the word about words. As people perceive that all about them things fall apart— education, the environment, the moral fabric—they are concerned to preserve and enlarge the hallmark of their humanness, and that hallmark is their language. To paraphrase Mark Twain, who makes an appearance in the middle of this book, rumors of the death of English are highly exaggerated.

Oh, yes: that telephone call. As succinctly as I could, I addressed my listener's inquiry. I told him that I was delighted with his question about *sheep* and *mutton* because it touched on a fascinating aspect of the history of our English language. In 1066 the Norman French invaded England and within a year ruled all of the country. The Norman Conquest signaled the end of the Old English period and the beginning of Middle English, but the French that the Norman nobility spoke did not reach down to the lower classes, the folk who, in the long run, were to determine the nature of our language.

This separation explains why live animals, which were tended by the Saxon peasants, had English names—*sheep*, *cow*, *ox*, *swine*, *calf*, *deer*, and *chicken*—while the animals that were "carried to the castle hall to feast among the nobles," as Walter Scott writes in *Ivanhoe*, had French names—*mutton*, *beef*, *pork*, *bacon*, *veal*, *venison*, and *pullet*.

All this took me about ten minutes to outline, and the tutorial made me late for the concert. I tore downstairs, jumped into my car, and sped toward the event. At the last major intersection before the junior high school, the car in front of me made a left, and I floated in behind it. Sure enough, as I arrived at the school parking lot, right behind me were the blue flashing lights of a police car. When I stopped, a young officer strode over to my automobile and said, "License and registration, please."

"Yes sir," I sighed and presented the documents.

"Do you know why I stopped you?" he asked.

Well, I knew, but I wanted him to say.

"Why did you stop me, officer?"

"Because you didn't come to a complete stop at the intersection of South Fruit and Clinton streets."

Sensing a redundancy aborning, I asked, "Well then, what did I do?"

"You only came to a partial stop."

Seizing on the oxymoron, I fixed him with a steely gaze. "Officer, what in the world is a partial stop?"

His head jerked back and he exclaimed, "Are you the guy who writes those books about language?"

I said I was and he let me off.

That's one of the advantages of being a "guy who writes those books about language." You intimidate people—and you save $33 on a traffic ticket.

Most people perceive us English teachers as prissy, fastidious characters, and being in the presence of a so-called language expert brings forth certain stock responses: "Gee, English was my worst subject in school. I hated diagramming sentences." Or: "So, you're an English teacher. I guess I'd better watch my grammar." Or: "You're the language person, eh. I'm afraid to say anything in your presence." To which I often want to reply, "Yeah, between you and I, you better speak and write good or I ain't gonna give you no respect irregardless!"

But those of us who truly cherish language are not linguistic sheriffs who organize posses to hunt down and string up language offenders who have the temerity or misfortune to split their infinitives, float their *hopefully*s, and dangle their participles in public. The last thing in the world we want to do is to make people uptight about the epicenter of their identity—the way they communicate. We celebrate language as the most glorious of all human inventions, incomparably the finest of our achievements. We marvel at the fact that, as you pass your eyes over the pages in this book, you experience ideas similar to those that I was thinking when, in another place and another time, I struck the symbols on my keyboard. Because I write and you read, we can both extend ourselves beyond the creatures we each were when we were born and the people we each were before I began the writing and you the reading.

If you are a genuine linguophile, an authentic logolept, and a certifiable verbivore, you are in for a lifetime of joy. You don't have to go to a special room like a laboratory or a theater or a special part of the country or the world to experience your delight. You have only to listen to the sounds that escape through the holes in people's faces and pay heed to the messages that flow from their pens and luminesce up on their computer screens. That is the stuff that this book is made on. That is the miracle that we call language.

RICHARD LEDERER
Concord, New Hampshire

I

WINGED WORDS

THE MIRACLE
OF LANGUAGE

"**L**anguage is the Rubicon that divides man from beast," declared the philologist Max Müller. The boundary between human and animal—between the most primitive savage and the highest ape—is the language line. In some tribes in Africa, a baby is called a *kuntu*, a "thing," not yet a *muntu*, a "person." It is only through the gift of language that the child acquires reason, the complexity of thought that sets him or her apart from the other creatures who share this planet. The birth of language is the dawn of humanity; in our beginning was the word. We have always been endowed with language because before we had words, we were not human beings.

"The limits of my language," wrote the philosopher Ludwig Wittgenstein, "are the limits of my mind. All I know is what I have words for." Without the word we are imprisoned; possessing the word, we are set free. Listen now to the stories of four thinkers—two men, two women; two whites, two blacks—as they give eloquent testimony to the emancipating power of language.

Most of us cannot remember learning our first word, but Helen Keller recalled that event in her life with a flashing vividness. She remembered because she was deaf, mute, and blind from the age of nineteen months and did not learn her first word until she was seven.

When Helen was six, an extraordinary teacher named Anne Mansfield Sullivan entered her life. Miss Sullivan was poor, ill, and nearly blind herself, but she possessed a tenacious vitality that was to force her pupil's unwilling mind from the dark, silent prison in which it lived: "Before my teacher came to me, I lived in a world that was a no-world. I cannot hope to describe adequately that unconscious yet conscious time of nothingness. I did not know that I knew aught, or that I lived or acted or desired."

In his play *The Miracle Worker*, William Gibson shows us what happened when Anne Sullivan first met Helen's mother:

MRS. KELLER: What will you try to teach her first?
ANNE SULLIVAN: First, last, and in between, language.
MRS. KELLER: Language.
ANNE SULLIVAN: Language is to the mind more than light is to the eye.

The miracle that Anne Sullivan worked was to give Helen Keller language, for only language could transform a small animal that looked like a child, a *kuntu*, into a human being, a *muntu*. Day after day, month after month, Anne Sullivan spelled words into Helen's hand. Finally, when Helen was seven years old and working with her teacher in the presence of water, she spoke her first word. Years later she described that moment in *The Story of My Life* (1902):

> Somehow the mystery of language was revealed to me. I knew then that "w-a-t-e-r" meant that wonderful cool something that was flowing over my hand. That living word awakened my soul, gave it light, hope, joy, set it free! . . . I left the well-house eager to learn. Everything had a name, and each name gave birth to a new thought.

Not only did Helen Keller learn to speak, write, and understand the English language. She graduated *cum laude* from Radcliffe College and went on to become a distinguished lecturer and writer. But perhaps the most poignant moment in her life came when, at the age of nine, she was able to say to Anne Sullivan, "I am not dumb now."

Richard Wright spent his childhood in the Jim Crow South—a prison of poverty, fear, and racism. He was born on a farm near Natchez, Mississippi, and, when he was five, his sharecropper father deserted the family. Richard, his mother, and his brother had to move from one community to another throughout the South so that he seldom remained in one school for an entire year. Yet somehow Richard Wright escaped the prison of hunger and hatred to become the most significant black writer in America, the author of *Native Son* (1940) and *Black Boy* (1945), two watershed books in American literature.

In *Black Boy*, Wright's unsparing autobiography, he describes his liberation at the age of eighteen. Because black people were not allowed library privi-

leges, Wright used the card of a friendly white man
along with a forged note that said, "Dear Madam: Will
you please let this nigger boy have some books by
H. L. Mencken." He obtained a copy of Mencken's *A
Book of Prefaces*, and all at once the sun of great
literature burst through the window of his prison:

> That night in my rented room, while letting the
> hot water run over my pork and beans in the sink, I
> opened *A Book of Prefaces* and began to read. I was
> jarred and shocked by the style, the clear, clean, sweep-
> ing sentences. Why did he write like that? And how
> did one write like that? . . . I stood up, trying to realize
> what reality lay behind the meaning of the words. Yes,
> this man was fighting with words. He was using words
> as a weapon, using them as one would use a club. . . .
> Then, maybe, perhaps, I could use them as a
> weapon. . . .
>
> What strange world was this? I concluded the
> book with the conviction that I had somehow over-
> looked something terribly important in life. I had once
> tried to write, had once reveled in feeling, had let my
> crude imagination roam, but the impulse to dream had
> been slowly beaten out of me by experience. Now it
> surged up again and I hungered for books, new ways
> of looking and seeing.

The titles of his first three works—*Uncle Tom's
Children*, *Native Son*, and *Black Boy*—keep alive the
abiding memory that Richard Wright always carried
for the child who opened a book by H. L. Mencken and
discovered a world, for the son who never felt himself
native to the country of his birth, and for the boy who

struggled out of the depths to speak for those who remained behind.

In *The Autobiography of Malcolm X* (1964), Malcolm tells how he rose from a world of thieving, pimping, and drug peddling to become one of the most articulate and dynamic leaders of the black revolution in America. Like Helen Keller and Richard Wright, Malcolm X was walled within a prison, in this instance the Norfolk Prison Colony, and, like them, he gained his liberation through the gift of language.

Frustrated by his inability to express himself in writing, Malcolm borrowed a dictionary from the prison school and slowly, painstakingly, began to copy—word by word and page by page—the entire dictionary onto his tablet: "With every succeeding page, I also learned of people and places and events from history. Actually the dictionary is like a miniature encyclopedia." As his vocabulary expanded, an already powerful speaker experienced a new empowerment through literacy. He read all day and even at night, in the faint glow of a corridor light:

> Anyone who has read a great deal can imagine the new world that opened up. Let me tell you something: from then until I left that prison, in every free moment I had, if I was not reading in the library, I was reading in my bunk. You couldn't have gotten me out of books with a wedge. . . . Months passed without my even thinking about being imprisoned. In fact, up to then, I had never been so truly free in my life.

The last of our four prisoners is Anne Frank, a young Jewish girl who grew up in Amsterdam during the Nazi occupation of Holland. In July of 1942 Anne's family was forced into hiding in the upper story of an Amsterdam warehouse, where they remained for twenty-five months. The rooms became more suffocating than any prison one could imagine. The Franks, who shared the space with another family and with an elderly dentist, were unable to feel the sun's warmth, unable to breathe fresh air. While the warehouse was in operation during the day, there could be no noise of any kind—no speaking, no unnecessary movements, no running of water.

Then, in 1944, the hideout was discovered by the police. Of the eight who had been crowded into the sealed-off attic rooms, only Mr. Frank survived the ensuing horrors of the concentration camps. In March 1945, two months before the liberation of Holland and three months before her sixteenth birthday, Anne Frank perished in the camp at Bergen-Belsen. According to one witness, she "died peacefully, feeling that nothing bad was happening to her."

Anne may have been devoured by the concentration camps, but her voice was not stilled. From the pages of a small, red-checkered, cloth-covered diary book, she speaks to us across the years. The diary was the favorite gift that Anne received for her thirteenth birthday. She named it Kitty and determined to express to her new confidante her innermost thoughts, concerns, and desires. Between the covers of Kitty the young girl, Anne Frank, recorded her moving commentary on war and its impact on human beings:

I see the eight of us with our "Secret Annexe" as if we were a little piece of blue heaven, surrounded by heavy black rain clouds. The round, clearly defined spot where we stand is still safe, but the clouds gather more closely about us and the circle which separates us from the approaching danger closes more and more tightly. Now we are so surrounded by danger and darkness that we bump against each other, as we search desperately for a means of escape. We all look down below, where people are fighting each other, we look above, where it is quiet and beautiful, and meanwhile we are cut off by the great dark mass, which will not let us go upwards, but which stands before us as an impenetrable wall; it tries to crush us, but cannot do so yet. I can only cry and implore: "Oh, if only the black circle could recede and open the way for us!"

Finally the Franks were betrayed, and on August 4, 1944, the fury of the Gestapo burst upon them. The invaders confiscated the silverware and Chanukah candlestick, but they threw the family's papers to the floor, including Anne's diary, which was recovered a year later by Mr. Frank.

The Nazis had failed in their mission. *Anne Frank: The Diary of a Young Girl* was first published in 1947 and has since been translated into tens of languages and sold millions of copies. No one has described its impact more eloquently than Anne's biographer, Ernst Schnabel: "Her voice was preserved out of the millions that were silenced, this voice no louder than a child's whisper. . . . It has outlasted the shouts of the murderers and soared above the voices of time."

What do the stories of Helen Keller, Richard Wright, Malcolm X, and Anne Frank say to us? They tell us that the world we perceive is the world we see through words. They tell us, as Wittgenstein once wrote, that "of what we cannot speak, we must be silent." They tell us that human beings grapple with the mystery of life by trying to find words to say what it is. They tell us that we must never take for granted the miracle of language.

HOW DO
WE KNOW
WHAT WE KNOW?

In his short story "The Great Automatic Grammatisator," British writer Roald Dahl creates a computer genius named Adolph Knipe, who makes an epiphanous discovery: "Then suddenly, he was struck by a powerful but simple little truth, and it was this: *That English grammar is governed by rules that are almost mathematical in their strictness!* Given the words, and given the sense of what is to be said, then there is only one correct order in which those words can be arranged." With this insight, Knipe invents an Automatic Grammatisator that spews out manuscript after manuscript of mass-market fiction. The machine is so successful in simulating the style of pulp stories and novels that it corners the writing market in England and pushes all creative human authors to the brink of starvation.

But Adolph Knipe is a character in a science-fiction story. In real life no linguist or computer expert has yet managed to build an "automatic grammatisator"— a device that can generate all, and only, the permissible sentences in English. Yet children do it all the time. In a remarkably short period they acquire a complex set of internalized rules, a feat that defies the most sophisticated of machines. Whatever the mechanical wonders of science, it is we human beings who are the great automatic grammatisators.

To begin with the most basic of questions, how do we ever learn what words are? Language is like a flowing stream sweeping onward with few discernible breaks in the flow. When we hear someone speaking a foreign language that we do not understand, we find that we cannot derive (Latin *de rivo*, "from the river") words from the ongoing speech stream. To an infant in the early stages of development, what ultimately becomes its native tongue is at first also a foreign language. Studies have shown that even for adults, who already have a vocabulary, thephysicalcuesthatdividespokenwordsarevagueandunreliable. Try, for examples, to stake out the boundaries between *no notion* and *known ocean*, *buys ink* and *buy zinc*, *meteorologist* and *meaty urologist*, and *cat's kills*, *cat skills*, and *Catskills*. How do we ever learn to pluck words, phrases, and clauses from the rushing river of speech?

Quite obviously, we do manage to isolate words, but how are we able to pair words with appropriate meanings? To illustrate how difficult this question is, consider the problems that a child confronts in determining something as seemingly simple as what the word *duck* means. On a first approximation, the child would simply have to notice that every time its mother emits the sound *duk*, there are ducks out in the world and make the connection between the object and the sound. The situation, however, is not that elementary. One complication is that the mother will use a word when the object to which that word refers is not present: "Let's go to the park and feed the ducks."

But even if the child could distinguish between instances in which the mother refers to the here and now as opposed to the then and there, he or she is still faced with enormous problems in figuring out what *duck* means. This is because the number of concepts consistent with the use of the word *duck* is infinite. The child could conjecture that *duck* means "animal" or "feathers" or "bird that swims" or "thing that goes quack," to name just a few possibilities. How is it that, in just a few trials, the child can figure out the meaning of the word *duck* that is consistent with the real-world conditions for its use?

Many words, of course, are more abstract than *duck* in that they have no referents in the physical world. Consider a verb like *think*, which refers to a mental act, something we cannot see, unless *think* happens to be uttered in front of the famous Rodin statue. How can the child deduce, just by looking out in the world, what the meaning of *think* is? What is it in the world that distinguishes thinking from other mental acts or states, like wanting, hoping, and liking? And how does the child grasp the meaning and use of even more abstract words, like *beyond*, *despite*, and *the*?

Even when we acquire our words and their meanings, how do we learn to string words together into statements? In order to speak, we humans must possess a highly complex set of internalized rules that enable us to utter any of (and only) the permissible sequences in a given language—although we are unlikely to have any conscious knowledge of the rules.

I'm thinking about a group of scholars. There are

five of them and I am concentrating on those particular five only. These scholars are from Lithuania, they are old, and they are scholars of Shakespeare. Now describe these men, using all the information I have just provided. Voilà! Your cluster of words is, almost certainly, "those five old Lithuanian Shakespearean scholars." Every native or experienced adult speaker of English knows to put the adjectives in the order above. How do we learn the exact order of that sequence—demonstrative pronoun-number-adjective-nationality-adjective-noun, marching in a line?

How do we come to separate what is a permissible phrase or sentence in English from what is unacceptable? How do we learn that we can say, "I don't have much money" but not "I have much money," "I don't think I can do it" but not "I think I can't do it," and "I am eating lunch" but not "I am knowing what is best for you"? We talk easily and naturally about a pole of ten feet and a crew of eight men, but how do we know that we must say, "a ten-foot pole" and "an eight-man crew," not "a ten-feet pole" and "an eight-men crew"? How do we know that "a friend of Paul" and "a friend of Paul's" mean the same thing, but "a picture of Paul" and "a picture of Paul's" mean different things? We learn that pronouns can represent nouns in almost any situation, as in "I looked the word up" and "I looked it up." But how do we learn that we can't replace "I looked up the word," with "I looked up it"?

Picture a building. Five feet from that building is parked a bicycle. Now state the relationship between the building and the bicycle, using the phrase "next to." Just about every reader of this book will say, "The bicycle is next to the building," rather than "The building is next to the bicycle." Yet in the physical world there is a reciprocal relationship in which the bicycle and the building are equidistant from each other. Apparently some internalized rule informs us that in such statements we place the more important object or person second in a sentence, in the same way that we know to say, "My sister met the Pope," rather than "The Pope met my sister." But who teaches us such a rule, and how do we learn it?

What does *wanna* mean? Easy, you reply: *Wanna* is a slurring or contraction of "want to," as *gonna* is a slurring of "going to" and *hafta* of "have to." Then, presumably, in all informal situations, *wanna* can be used interchangeably with "want to." But consider these two sentences: "There goes the man I wanna banish" and "There goes the man I wanna vanish." As accomplished speakers of English we hear that the second sentence is unnatural and non-native. We sense that the construction "There goes the man I wanna . . ." works only with verbs that take objects— "There goes the man I wanna see"; "There goes the woman I wanna meet"—but not with intransitive verbs that do not act upon objects—"There goes the man I wanna become"; "There goes the woman I wanna laugh." (Thus, "There goes the woman I wanna win" and "There goes the man I wanna eat" make sense in English only if the first speaker wants to win the woman and the second speaker is a cannibal.) Whether or not we have intellectually mastered the intricacies of distinguishing transitive from intransitive verbs, we know exactly when we can and cannot use them in a sentence. Even if we have never studied the "rules" of grammar in school, we automatic grammatisators know them, deep down in the circuitry of our brains.

What do we know about languaging that we do not know we know?

For most of us, language is like the air we breathe. Like air, language is invisible and all around us. We need it to live, yet we take it for granted. If, however, we pause and examine our speaking and writing thoughtfully, we discover that the ordinary language user is astonishingly creative. Without realizing it, we all spend most of our waking hours inventing language.

Incredible as it may seem at first thought, practically every sentence that you speak and write during your lifetime has never been spoken or written before in human history. Except for stock phrases and conventional remarks, such as "How are you?", "Thanks a lot," and "Have a nice day," almost all of your speech and writing consists of sentences that you have made up. You are a language inventor.

Consider, for example, an experiment conducted by Richard Ohmann, a professor at Wesleyan University, who placed before twenty-five people a fairly simple cartoon and asked them to describe in a sentence the situation the drawing portrayed. Not surprisingly, the twenty-five descriptions that Professor Ohmann received were all different:

> "A bear is occupying a phone booth, while a tourist impatiently waits in line."
> "A man who was driving along the road has stopped and is waiting impatiently for a grizzly bear to finish using the public phone."
> "A traveler waits impatiently as a bear chatters gaily in a highway telephone booth."

Then Professor Ohmann used a computer to determine how many grammatical sentences in English could be generated from the raw materials in just those twenty-five sentences about the agitated tourist and the bear in the telephone booth.

How many would you guess? Five thousand? Ten thousand? Maybe twenty-five thousand?

Professor Ohmann's computer yielded 19.8 billion!—nearly twenty billion English sentences that depict one limited state of affairs culled from only twenty-five different statements. 19.8 billion is a very large number. In fact, it would take about forty human life spans to speak 19.8 billion sentences, even at high speed.

Other computer studies have shown that it would take ten trillion years—two thousand times the estimated age of the earth—to utter all the possible English sentences that use exactly twenty words. Therefore, it is highly unlikely that any twenty-word sentence an individual speaks has ever been spoken previously. The same conclusion holds true, of course, for sentences of greater length and for most shorter sentences as well. That is why almost every sentence that you are reading in this book, as well as in all the books, newspapers, and magazines that have been written and are yet to be written, is expressed, or will be expressed, in its exact form for the very first time.

There is one more intriguing fact to consider. Not only do you spend your days reading sentences that you have never before encountered, but you understand almost every one of them. Part of your humanness is your ability both to invent new sentences and to comprehend the verbal inventions of other people. Linguist Noam Chomsky maintains that "when we study human language, we are approaching what some might call 'the human essence,' the distinct qualities of mind that are, so far as we know, unique to man." If you fill your speech and writing with prefabricated clichés, ramshackle abstractions, and leaden expressions, you are denying the abounding creativity that is inherent in the very nature of human language. Thus it is that the manner in which you utter words, write words, and receive words throughout your life determines how effectively and resourcefully you carry on the business of being a member of the human race.

IN PRAISE OF ENGLISH

In the year 1599, the poet and historian Samuel Daniel sang of the English language that was coming to full flower during the Elizabethan Age:

> And who, in time, knows whither we may vent
>> The treasure of our tongue, to what strange shores
> This gaine of our best glory shall be sent.
>> T'inrich unknowing Nations with our stores?
> What words in the yet unformed Occident
>> May come refined with the accents that are ours?

The answer to Samuel Daniel's questions is that English, "the treasure of our tongue," has been transported around the globe and has become the most widely spoken language in the history of humankind, the linguistic wonder of the modern world.

The Académie Française has announced, with typical Gallic precision, that there are 2,796 languages existing today. Of these, only ten are the native tongue

19

of more than a hundred million people. Chinese boasts more than a billion native speakers, English 350 million, and then, according to Charles Berlitz in *Native Tongues*, in descending order come Hindustani, Russian, Spanish, Japanese, German, Indonesian, Portuguese, and French.

Although Chinese surpasses English in the sheer number of its native speakers, it does not rival English as a global language. One may legitimately ask if Chinese is indeed a single language, as it is subdivided into five distinct dialects that are mutually unintelligible in their spoken forms. While Chinese is largely concentrated in its populous homeland and ethnic enclaves, English is spoken all over the planet by people of all races and nearly all religions and cultures. In fact, recent surveys indicate that those using English as a preferred second language outnumber those who use it natively.

English is the first or official language of forty-five countries covering one-fifth of the earth's land surface. More than ten percent of the populations of other countries, such as India, Pakistan, Malaysia, Switzerland, Holland, Denmark, and Sweden, are able to converse in English. One out of every seven people in the world understands and speaks the English language in some form.

The majority of the world's books, newspapers, and magazines are written in English. Most international telephone calls are made in English. Sixty percent of the world's radio programs are beamed in English, and more than seventy percent of international mail and seventy-five percent of cable messages and telexes are written and addressed in English. It is the language in which two-thirds of all scientific treatises and technical periodicals are printed and eighty percent of all computer text stored.

The rise of English as a planetary language is an unparalleled success story that begins long ago, in the middle of the fifth century A.D. At the onset of the Dark Ages, several large tribes of sea rovers, the Angles, Saxons, and Jutes, lived along the continental North Sea coast, from Denmark to Holland. They were a fierce warrior people who built beaked galleys and fought with huge battle-axes and battle hammers, burning towns and carrying off anything they happened to want. Around A.D. 449, these Teutonic plunderers sailed across the water and invaded the islands then known as Britannia. They found the land pleasant and the people, fighting among themselves, very easy to conquer, and so they remained there. They brought with them a Low Germanic tongue that, in its new setting, became Anglo-Saxon, or Old English, the ancestor of the English we use today. During the reign of King Egbert in the ninth century, the land became known as *Englaland*, "the land of the Angles," and the language *Englisc*, because the Angles were at that time the chief group.

A dramatic evolution in the language came after yet another conquest of England, this one by the Norman French two centuries after the rule of Egbert. The new conquerors came from Normandy, a province of France on the other side of the English Channel. These people had been Vikings and freebooters from the Scandinavian countries who spoke French and had taken to French customs. Their *triouveurs*, or minstrels, sang the *Song of Roland* and the legends of the earlier Frankish king Charlemagne.

In 1066, under William, Duke of Normandy, the

Normans invaded England. In a bloody battle at Hastings they conquered the Saxons and Danes who resisted them, killed Saxon King Harold, and forced the nobles to choose Duke William as king of England. One would quite naturally suppose that the language of England would thus come to be French with only a sprinkling of Anglo-Saxon, but almost the opposite happened. As the invaders, far outnumbered by their captives, lost their ties to France, they took to English as easily as their Norman forebears had dropped their Norse speech for French. Many of their French words entered the vocabulary of their adopted tongue, and the changing language evolved into a form we now call Middle English.

Meanwhile, Latin words crept into the English language for many centuries, beginning with the Roman conquest of England in the first century B.C. by Julius Caesar and the influence of the Roman church and missionaries a few centuries later. But the mightiest infusion of Latin words into the great river of English came after the Norman Conquest, either through Norman French or directly from Latin.

The European Renaissance, from the fourteenth into the seventeenth century, began as educated men and women rediscovered the world of ancient Greece and Rome, a world that had been partly shrouded by the darkness of the Middle Ages. The Renaissance was a love affair with anything classical, including all manner of Latin and Greek words, especially those that could name and describe the new discoveries that were bursting forth in science, medicine, art, literature, and world geography. Because these classical words entered the English language primarily through writing, often scholarly writing, they are the kind that we use formally rather than in everyday conversation.

The result of this mingled history is a distinctive three-tiered vocabulary of Anglo-Saxon, French, and classical synonyms that offer us at least three choices for conveying approximately the same meaning. A sampling of these triplets reveals how we can play the music of English with considerably more than one string at just the register we deem most appropriate:

Anglo-Saxon	French	Latin/Greek
ask	question	interrogate
dead	deceased	defunct
end	finish	conclude
fair	beautiful	attractive
fear	terror	trepidation
help	aid	assist
rise	mount	ascend
thin	spare	emaciated

Bequeathing us the common words of everyday life, many of them fashioned from a single syllable, Anglo-Saxon is the foundation of our language. Its directness, brevity, and plainness make us feel more deeply and see things about us more truly. The grandeur, sonority, and courtliness of the French elements lift us to another, and more literary, level of expression. At the third tier, the precision and learnedness of our Greek and Latin vocabulary arouse our minds to more complex thinking and the making of fine distinctions.

During the age of Elizabeth I and Shakespeare, the time when Samuel Daniel wrote his poem, English was the mother tongue of only five to seven million speakers tucked away on a foggy island in Western Europe. One of Daniel's contemporaries noted that the language was "of small reatch, it stretcheth no further than this iland of ours, naie not there over all." English was outstripped by French, German, Spanish, and Italian; today it has almost as many speakers as the four put together. Why is it that English has grown a hundredfold in the space of the four centuries that have intervened since the Renaissance? How is it that English has become such a mighty instrument, the most formidable contender for the honor of world tongue?

The emergence of England and then the United States as economic, military, and scientific superpowers has, of course, contributed to the phenomenal spread of the English language. But the essential reasons for the ascendancy of English lie in the internationality of its words and the relative simplicity of its grammar and syntax.

It is often said that what most immediately sets English apart from other languages is the richness of its vocabulary. *Webster's Third New International Dictionary* lists 450,000 words, and the compendious *Oxford English Dictionary* lists 615,000, but that is only part of the total. Technical and scientific terms, family words, slang and argot, and spanking-new creations, unenshrined in ordinary dictionaries, would add hundreds of thousands more, bringing the total of entries to as high as two million. In comparison, German, according to traditional estimates, has a vocabulary of about 185,000, Russian 130,000, and French fewer than 100,000.

One reason English has accumulated such a vast word hoard is that it is the most hospitable and democratic language that has ever existed. English has never rejected a word because of its race, creed, or national origin. Having welcomed into its vocabulary words from a multitude of other languages and dialects, ancient and modern, far and near, English is unique in the number and variety of its borrowed words. Fewer than thirty percent of our words spring from the original Anglo-Saxon word stock; the rest are imported. As the poet Carl Sandburg once said, "The English language hasn't got where it is by being pure."

Joseph Bellafiore has described the English language as "the lagoon of nations" because "in it there are hundreds of miscellaneous words floating like ships from foreign ports freighted with messages for us." The three largest of those galleons are Latin (from which we derive the likes of *circus*), Greek (*drama*), and French (*garage*). Although Anglo-Saxon is the foundation of the English language, more than seventy percent of our words have been imported from other lands. To appreciate how cosmopolitan is the word-bearing fleet docked in the wide lagoon of English, examine the following list of fifty familiar English words, along with the languages from which they descend:

aardvark: Afrikaans	*polka:* Czech
moose: Algonquin	*teepee:* Dakota
alcohol: Arabic	*skill:* Danish
poncho: Arauncanian	*boss:* Dutch
boomerang: Australian	*oasis:* Egyptian
zebra: Bantu	*sauna:* Finnish
anchovy: Basque	*kindergarten:* German
bungalow: Bengali	*jaguar:* Guarani
typhoon: Cantonese	*jukebox:* Gullah
hurricane: Carib	*canoe:* Haitian creole
Eskimo: Cree	*ukulele:* Hawaiian

camel: Hebrew	*bazaar:* Persian
saber: Hungarian	*mazurka:* Polish
whisk: Icelandic	*molasses:* Portuguese
banshi: Irish	*pal:* Romany
opera: Italian	*vodka:* Russian
tycoon: Japanese	*sugar:* Sanskrit
batik: Javanese	*rodeo:* Spanish
tundra: Lapp	*smorgasbord:* Swedish
bantam: Malagasi	*boondocks:* Tagalog
ketchup: Malay	*tattoo:* Tahitian
kiwi: Maori	*polo:* Tibetan
coyote: Mexican Indian	*jackal:* Turkish
shingle: Norwegian	*flannel:* Welsh
wigwam: Ojibwa	*kibitzer:* Yiddish

No wonder Ralph Waldo Emerson waxed ecstatic about "English speech, the sea which receives tributaries from every region under heaven" and Dorothy Thompson, employing a more prosaic metaphor, referred to "that glorious and imperial mongrel, the English language." With its liberal borrowing policy, English is easy to learn because it has a familiar look to speakers of other languages. And, by taking in and completely assimilating so many alien words, English has accumulated the most versatile of all vocabularies. Sir Philip Sidney, the quintessential Elizabethan—at once poet, courtier, and soldier—celebrated this word-wealth: "But for the uttering sweetly and properly the conceite of the minde . . . which is the ende of thought . . . English hath it equally with any other tongue in the world." Sidney saw how the abundance of synonyms and near synonyms in our language offers wondrous possibilities for the precise and complete expression of diverse shadings of meaning.

A recent *New Yorker* cartoon puckishly pointed up this treasure trove. The cartoon's caption read "Roget's Brontosaurus," and pictured was a big dinosaur in whose thought bubble appeared: "large, great, huge, considerable, bulky, voluminous, ample, massive, capacious, spacious, mighty, towering, monstrous . . ." Had there been more room, the artist could have added: "vast, enormous, tremendous, gigantic, weighty, sizable, substantial, lumbering, looming, jumbo, leviathan, mountainous, whopping, ponderous, prodigious, colossal, hulking, hefty, husky, humongous." Such a cartoon would be far less likely to appear in a magazine printed in a language other than English. Books like *Roget's Thesaurus* are foreign to speakers of most foreign languages; given the scope and structure of their vocabularies, they have little need of them.

Writer Michael Arlen calls English "the great Wurlitzer of language, the most perfect all-purpose instrument," but, as elaborate as its keyboard is, it is a relatively easy instrument to learn how to play. English possesses a fairly simple, stripped-down apparatus of grammar unencumbered by complex noun and adjective inflections and gender markers. (Even as I write this chapter the French are debating whether the word *microchip* should be masculine or feminine.) People often say to me that English must be a very arduous and intimidating language for foreigners to master. How difficult can it be, I answer, when more than 350 million second-language users have learned to speak and understand it? One of these come-latelies to English, Hungarian-born Stephen Baker, tells in *Writer's Digest* of his love for his adopted language:

> No doubt, English was invented in heaven. It must be the lingua franca of the angels.

No other language is like it. Nothing comes even close to it in sound, eloquence, and just plain common sense—and this from someone who spoke nary a word of it before reaching age twenty-five, save for *Coke*, *OK*, and *drugstore*. . . .

You will be surprised to hear me say this: English is probably among the easiest languages to learn—because grammatically it makes sense. Anyone who tells you it isn't should take a trip around the world and listen to tongues wagging. He'll be happy to come home again.

The great nineteenth-century linguist Jakob Grimm wrote, "In richness, good sense, and terse convenience, no other living language may be put beside English." By "terse convenience" Grimm meant that ours is a strikingly direct and concise tongue. Translate a document from English into French or Spanish or German or Russian, and the translation, if true to the original, will emerge about twenty-five percent longer. Examine bilingual signs and messages, and you will find that the English half is inevitably more compact. In the bathroom of a Toronto hotel in which I stayed are posted these messages, which I reproduce in their exact form:

CONSERVE
PRECIOUS
ENERGY

You can help conserve an adequate supply of energy for all by turning off TV and lights before leaving

CONSERVEZ
CETTE
PRECIEUSE
ENERGIE

Vous pouvez aider à assurer à tous des approvisionnements énergétiques suffisants en arrêtant le

your room; and by keeping windows closed when heat or air conditioning is on.	téléviseur et en éteignant les lampes avant de quitter la pièce; et en gardant les fenêtres bien fermées lorsque le chauffage ou la climatisation est en marche.

A careful count of the number of syllables needed to translate the Gospel according to Mark into various languages indicates that, compared to other tongues, brevity is the soul of English:

English	29,000
Teutonic languages (average)	32,650
French	36,500
Slavic languages (average)	36,500
Romance languages (average)	40,200
Indo-Iranian languages (average)	43,100

Although scientists haven't yet discovered the phenomenon, planet Earth is spinning with "reverse English." The language that was forged from invasion has itself become an invader on a global scale. The very English that through the centuries has imported so many words from so many other languages is today one of the world's most popular exports. Through its contributions to other tongues English is beginning to repay its historical debts and establish a linguistic balance of trade.

Pilots and air controllers in all international airports use English to communicate. English lyrics pervade rock music the world over. India, with almost two hundred different languages, relies on English to unify itself. From Athens to Baghdad, from Finland to Kabul, people stand in long lines to sign up for English classes that are vastly oversubscribed.

In a 1990 *New York Times* article, "English Uber Alles," Enno von Lowenstern, deputy editor of the German newspaper *Die Welt*, demonstrated that he could write an article in German in which the nouns were almost exclusively English. The piece began: "Unser Way of Life im Media Business ist hart, da muss man ein tougher Kerl sein. Morgens Warm-up und Stretching, dann ein Teller Corn Flakes und ein Soft Drink oder Darjeeling Tea, dann in das office— und schon Brunch mit den Top-Leuten, Meeting zum Thema: Sollen wir die Zeitung pushen mit Snob Appeal oder auf Low Profile achten?" If you were to read German newspapers, you would recognize English words such as *Scoop, Holiday, Paperbacks, Teenagers, Blue Jeans, Cowboys and Indians, Toasters,* and *Mixers,* as well as the sports terms *Ref, Goalkeeper, Puck, Body Check, Punch,* and *Boxing.*

American words have infiltrated even Russian stores with products like *miksers, tosters, komputers,* and *antifriz,* reflecting the fact that half of all foreign language classes in the Soviet Union are courses in English. By popular Soviet request, the British Broadcasting Corporation is supplying Moscow Radio with a series of programs emphasizing the essential English vocabulary of a capitalist society. To help Soviet listeners tell a stock from a bond and a bull from a bear, the BBC–Moscow Radio broadcasts encourage familiarity with such words and phrases as *collateral, management buyouts, export guarantees, Let's talk about that over lunch,* and *Do we have a deal?* In 1990, for the first time since Fidel Castro took over Cuba, English was taught in that country's elementary schools. Castro reportedly said about the role of English in Cuban education: "Although we might not like it, it's a universal language, the most widespread—much easier to learn than Russian and more precise above all in technical matters."

Many a Japanese businessman has a *kakuteiru* ("cocktail"), perhaps a *jintonikku* ("gin and tonic"), with his *fantazikku garu-furendo* ("fantastic girl friend"). For a snack later in the evening the couple might choose to have *aisukurimu* or *yoguruto*. If you're not sure what *aisukurimu* and *yoguruto* are, consider that they come in a variety of flavors, among them *chokoreto, banira,* and *sutoroberi*.

Japanese ads, posters, and shopping bags are filled with a wiggy kind of American *Ingurisshu* ("English"): "World Smell in Cup Full," "Imagine Folkloric Sports in Summer," "My Life. My Gas," "Just Fit to You, King Kong." A number of these slogans start with an enthusiastic "Let's," as in "Let's Hiking," and "Let's Sports Violent All Day Long." Adorning Japanese clothing, pencil cases, and stationery are messages that also illustrate with charming absurdity the Japanese fascination with English: "Happy Good Day," "Fancy Pimple," and "Persistent Pursuit of Dainty."

The influx of English, especially American English, is not always welcomed abroad with open mouths. The French, who in 1635 formed the Académie Française for the purpose of trying to keep the language pure, have erected sea walls against the flood tide of *la langue du Coca-Cola,* as they call American English. They are battling what they consider to be a gypsy moth infestation by such Americanisms as *le drugstore, skyscraper, weekend, shopping, parking, rafting, fast food, jumbo jet,* and *quick lunch,* all in common usage in France. In 1989 the Pasteur Institute of Paris decided to rename three of its most important scientific journals and publish them in English. The Académie Française, composed of forty intellectuals, urged the Pasteur Institute to rescind its decision, which it termed "a demonstration of the unjustified surrender of a part of the French scientific community." The Institute hasn't backed down.

The English language continues to be one of the world's great growth industries, adding more than a thousand new words a year to its word store and, since World War II, garnering new speakers at an annual rate of about two percent. Over the course of a millennium and a half, it has evolved from the rude tongue of a few isolated Germanic tribes into an international medium of exchange in science, commerce, politics, diplomacy, tourism, literature, and pop culture—the closest thing we have ever had to a global language. If ever our descendants make contact with articulate beings from other planets and other solar systems, English will doubtless start adding and assimilating words from Martian, Saturnian, and Alpha Centaurian and beaming its vocabulary across outer space. Then English will become a truly universal language.

THE CASE FOR SHORT WORDS

When you speak and write, there is no law that says you have to use big words. Short words are as good as long ones, and short, old words—like *sun* and *grass* and *home*—are best of all. A lot of small words, more than you might think, can meet your needs with a strength, grace, and charm that large words do not have.

Big words can make the way dark for those who read what you write and hear what you say. Small words cast their clear light on big things—night and day, love and hate, war and peace, and life and death. Big words at times seem strange to the eye and the ear and the mind and the heart. Small words are the ones we seem to have known from the time we were born, like the hearth fire that warms the home.

Short words are bright like sparks that glow in the night, prompt like the dawn that greets the day, sharp like the blade of a knife, hot like salt tears that scald the cheek, quick like moths that flit from flame to flame, and terse like the dart and sting of a bee.

Here is a sound rule: Use small, old words where you can. If a long word says just what you want to say, do not fear to use it. But know that our tongue is rich in crisp, brisk, swift, short words. Make them the spine and the heart of what you speak and write. Short words are like fast friends. They will not let you down.

The title of this chapter and the four paragraphs that you have just read are wrought entirely of words of one syllable. In setting myself this task, I did not feel especially cabined, cribbed, or confined. In fact, the structure helped me to focus on the power of the message I was trying to put across.

One study shows that twenty words account for twenty-five percent of all spoken English words, and all twenty are monosyllabic. In order of frequency they are: *I, you, the, a, to, is, it, that, of, and, in, what, he, this, have, do, she, not, on,* and *they.* Other studies indicate that the fifty most common words in written English are each made of a single syllable.

For centuries our finest poets and orators have recognized and employed the power of small words to make a straight point between two minds. A great many of our proverbs punch home their points with pithy monosyllables: "Where there's a will, there's a way," "A stitch in time saves nine," "Spare the rod and spoil the child," "A bird in the hand is worth two in the bush."

Nobody used the short word more skillfully than William Shakespeare, whose dying King Lear laments:

And my poor fool is hang'd! No, no, no life!
Why should a dog, a horse, a rat have life,

And thou no breath at all? . . .
Do you see this? Look on her, look, her lips.
Look there, look there!

Shakespeare's contemporaries made the King James Bible a centerpiece of short words—"And God said, Let there be light: and there was light. And God saw the light, that it was good." The descendants of such mighty lines live on in the twentieth century. When asked to explain his policy to Parliament, Winston Churchill responded with these ringing monosyllables: "I will say: it is to wage war, by sea, land, and air, with all our might and with all the strength that God can give us." In his "Death of the Hired Man" Robert Frost observes that "Home is the place where, when you go there,/They have to take you in." And William H. Johnson uses ten two-letter words to explain his secret of success: "If it is to be,/It is up to me."

You don't have to be a great author, statesman, or philosopher to tap the energy and eloquence of small words. Each winter I ask my ninth graders at St. Paul's School to write a composition composed entirely of one-syllable words. My students greet my request with obligatory moans and groans, but, when they return to class with their essays, most feel that, with the pressure to produce high-sounding polysyllables relieved, they have created some of their most powerful and luminous prose. Here are submissions from two of my ninth graders:

> What can you say to a boy who has left home? You can say that he has done wrong, but he does not care. He has left home so that he will not have to deal with what you say. He wants to go as far as he can. He will do what he wants to do.

This boy does not want to be forced to go to church, to comb his hair, or to be on time. A good time for this boy does not lie in your reach, for what you have he does not want. He dreams of ripped jeans, shorts with no starch, and old socks.

So now this boy is on a bus to a place he dreams of, a place with no rules. This boy now walks a strange street, his long hair blown back by the wind. He wears no coat or tie, just jeans and an old shirt. He hates your world, and he has left it.—*Charles Shaffer*

For a long time we cruised by the coast and at last came to a wide bay past the curve of a hill, at the end of which lay a small town. Our long boat ride at an end, we all stretched and stood up to watch as the boat nosed its way in.

The town climbed up the hill that rose from the shore, a space in front of it left bare for the port. Each house was a clean white with sky blue or grey trim; in front of each one was a small yard, edged by a white stone wall strewn with green vines.

As the town basked in the heat of noon, not a thing stirred in the streets or by the shore. The sun beat down on the sea, the land, and the back of our necks, so that, in spite of the breeze that made the vines sway, we all wished we could hide from the glare in a cool, white house. But, as there was no one to help dock the boat, we had to stand and wait.

At last the head of the crew leaped from the side and strode to a large house on the right. He shoved the door wide, poked his head through the gloom, and roared with a fierce voice. Five or six men came out, and soon the port was loud with the clank of chains and creak of planks as the men caught ropes thrown by the crew, pulled them taut, and tied them to posts. Then they set up a rough plank so we could cross from the deck to the shore. We all made for the large house while the crew watched, glad to be rid of us.—*Celia Wren*

You too can tap into the vitality and vigor of compact expression. Take a suggestion from the highway department. At the boundaries of your speech and prose place a sign that reads "Caution: Small Words at Work."

ENGLISH AT PLAY

Having grown too old to ring the bell in the cathedral tower, Quasimodo, the hunchback of Notre Dame, ran an ad in the local newspaper for a replacement.

An armless man appeared at Quasimodo's door, and the old ring-master asked him, "Are you here for the job of bell ringer?"

"Yes, I am."

"But how can you ring the bell when you have no arms?"

"That's easy. I may lack arms, but I possess an extremely tough skull. I simply run at the bell and strike it with my forehead. The tone produced is absolutely exquisite."

"All right," conceded Quasimodo and hired the fellow.

The man ascended the spiral staircase, climbed into the bell tower, ran at the bell, and struck it with his forehead, indeed making a lovely clang. Alas, though, the bell swung back pendularly, smashed into the poor chap, and knocked him out of the tower. He splatted on the cobblestones far below.

When the police arrived at the scene, an officer asked, "Mr. Quasimodo, do you know this man?"

"Yes, I do," answered Quasi. "He was an employee of mine."

"For our records, please give us his name."

Quasimodo furrowed his brow. "I don't know his name, but his face rings a bell."

Shortly thereafter, Quasimodo placed a second ad in the paper asking for new bell-ringing applicants. A second gentleman appeared who looked exactly like the first, including the state of armlessness.

Quasimodo asked the new man, "Are you here for the position of bell ringer?"

"Yes, I am," replied the second man.

"Then I have two questions for you. First, am I wrong or do you look exactly like another fellow who was recently in my employ and who came to a tragic end?"

"That man was my older brother," replied the applicant. "Indeed, many people have remarked that I look just like him."

"You look so much like him," Quasimodo went on, "that you too lack arms. How do you propose to ring the bell?"

"Easy. Like my brother, I too have an exceedingly tough forehead, which I use to ring the bell, but I am more agile than my brother, and I have learned to get out of the way of the bell's backswing."

"Fine," sighed Quasimodo with relief. "You may start immediately."

The second gentleman mounted the spiral staircase, climbed up to the tower, and ran headlong into the bell, producing as exquisite a tone as had his brother. As the bell swayed back toward him, he deftly stepped aside and avoided getting clobbered by the return swing.

Alas, though, three nights later, the new bell ringer got stinking drunk. He staggered up the spiral staircase, lurched toward the bell, and struck it with his forehead. As he stood there swaying, the bell swung back and knocked him out of the tower and onto the cobblestones below.

Again the police arrived. "Do you know *this* man, Mr. Quasimodo?"

"Yes, he too was an employee of mine," answered the hunchback.

"May we have his name, please?"

"I don't know his name either, but he's a dead ringer for his brother."

You have just been the victim of two set-up puns, a conspiracy of narrative and multiple meanings. In this instance the wordplay is homographic: a word or expression—"his face rings a bell" and "dead ringer"—generates two or more different meanings.

Blessed with such a vast vocabulary and relatively unencumbered by word forms that petrify the parts of speech, English is one of the most playful languages that has ever cavorted across the planetary stage. We English speakers dance with words that are spelled and pronounced the same but have different meanings (*bat*, the mammal, and *bat*, as used in baseball), words that sound similar but not the same ("you're a sight for soirées"), words that are spelled the same but are different words with different sounds ("the entrance to the castle will entrance you"), words that spark off two opposite meanings (when the stars are out, they are visible; when the lights are out, they are invisible), words that contain different spellings and opposite meanings (*raised* and *razed*), words that change meaning when they leap from one part of speech to another (as one frog said to the other, "Time's fun when you're having flies"), and words that yield other words when sounds or syllables are reversed ("I'd rather have a bottle in front of me than a frontal lobotomy").

English is a veritable playground of words—words clambering over jungle gyms, words bouncing up and down on seesaws, words swinging on rings and ringing on swings, words whizzing down sliding boards, words merrily whirling around on merry-go-rounds. Many of our words and expressions were born in the playground of punnery. Have you ever wondered how we got the expression *funny bone?* Technically it is the ulnar nerve that causes that tingly sensation when we strike our arm, but the source of that feeling is the enlarged knob on the end of the bone running from the shoulder to the elbow. The medical name for that particular bone is the humerus, and back in 1840 some wag seized upon the homophonic similarity of *humerus* and *humorous* and dubbed the humerus the funny bone, a learned pun that has become part of our language.

One of the brightest and most pyrotechnic delights of the English language reposes in its uncommon stockpile of homophones, words that are spelled differently but pronounced the same. Have you heard the one about the man who bequeathed his offspring a cattle ranch and named it Focus?—because it was the place where the sons raise meat.

Hears a rye peace eye maid up inn my idol thyme.
Aye rote it four yew two sea Howe homophones
Cannes seam sew whiled from there knows down too
they're tows. With pried, eye no it will knot boar ewe.
Its meant two bee red allowed:

> One night a knight on a hoarse horse
>   Rode out upon a road.
> This male wore mail for war and would
>   Explore a wood that glowed.
>
> His tale I'll tell from head to tail.
>   I'll write his rite up right.
> A hidden site our hero found,
>   A sight that I shall cite.
>
> With woe he shouted, "Whoa!" as rain
>   Without a break did reign.
> To brake, he pulled the rein, and like
>   A shattered pane, felt pain.
>
> The poor knight met a witch, which made
>   Sweat pour from every pore.
> He'd never seen a scene like that.
>   His sore heart couldn't soar.
>
> Then they a game for truffles played,
>   In which he mined her mind.
> To prove who was the better bettor
>   And find who should be fined.
>
> He won one twice, he won two, too.
>   To grate on her felt great.
> To wrest the rest, he went for four,
>   And, at the fore, ate eight.

Due to her loss, the mourning witch,
  'Midst morning mist and dew,
Her truffles missed. I know no way,
  Do I, to weigh her rue.

The razed field raised our brave knight's fear,
  As a swarm of scared fleas flees.
He heard a herd of dear deer pray
  The pleas of prey: "Please, please."

A grisly grizzly bear, all bare,
  And a hare that had no hair
And a foul fowl bawled that they were bald.
  In their pink skins they stood there.

The knight did see a blue whale wail
  As it blew out plumes of sea.
"Yoo hoo, you who come riding here,
  Please hear and pity me."

Our knight began to reel, for real.
  The world whirled, so to speak.
All the days of the week his sole soul felt
  The dizzy daze of the weak.

Our heir to knighthood gave it up.
  He felt the fare not fair.
His wholly holy sword soared up
  As he threw it through the air.

The bell has tolled, I'm told. The hour
  To end our tale draws nigh.
Without ado, I bid adieu,
  So by your leave, bye-bye.

BRAVE NEW WORDS OF THE 1980S

A *baby boomer* (we'll call her Boomer for short), tired of life in the *fast track* spent *networking* with *yuppies, yumpies,* and *dinks,* disconnected her *cellular phone* and paid some *megabucks* to go to a *fat farm.* Feeling like a *couch potato,* she stopped her *feeding frenzies* with *calzone* and *chimi-changa* and gave the *high five* to *grazing* on *nouvelle cuisine.*

As newly minted words added to the currency of the language of the *wicked awesome* 1980s, Boomer had become confused with a world in which the parts of speech and meanings of words had transmogrified under her very eyes and ears. *FAX, Fedex,* and *microwave* had turned into verbs, and Bill Murray got *slimed* in the 1984 blockbuster *Ghostbusters.* A *hunk* no longer meant simply a large lump of something, and *channeling* became a new medium. *Crack* meant more than just a small opening and *ice* more than frozen water. A *pocket* wasn't just for pants, a *bar code* was no longer just ethics for lawyers or the etiquette of

44

behavior in a café, and *rap* wasn't just '60s talk. *Zapping* was not something that futuristic ray guns did but something that people did with a microwave or a television remote control. A *set point* was no longer just a tennis score, and *spin* was not just what a tennis ball did, especially in the hands of the *spin doctors*. A *pound* was no longer just a unit of currency or measurement but, in the words of James J. Kilpatrick, my colleague in columny, "the little thingamajig above the 3 on a standard typewriter or computer keyboard. It looks like a blank tic tac toe game that has had too much to drink." *CDs* were no longer just certificates, and *PC* had come to signify both "personal computer" and "politically correct." In fact, the computer had thoroughly befuddled her sense of *back up*, *bit*, *boot*, *crash*, *disk*, *hacker*, *mail*, *memory*, *menu*, *mouse*, *park*, *scroll*, *virus*, and *window*. No wonder that Boomer began feeling like a *no-brainer gomer*, a totally *loose cannon*, and a *ditzy airhead*.

As the *Me Generation* (a label invented by writer Tom Wolfe) grew up, our disoriented Boomer found that the business of America appeared to be business, and the business of business was to devise a lexicon of new terms to describe new fiscal realities. Courtesy of President Reagan (who gave us a new use of *Teflon*), we entered an era of *Reaganomics*, *supply-side* and *trickle-down* economics, and *Laffer curves*. The 1980s were a "golden" age of commerce—*golden handshakes*, *golden hellos*, and *golden parachutes*. The increasingly *proactive* world of business also gave us *automatic tellers*, *baby Bells*, *debit cards*, *entry level*, *intrapreneurs*, *pink collar*, *power breakfasts*, *power lunches*, and *power ties*, *program trading*, *quality circles*, *queen bees*, *telemarketing*, and *white knights*.

But Boomer found that life among the *movers and shakers* was fraught with the perils of *greenmail*, *hostile takeovers*, *junk bonds*, *leveraged buyouts*, and *poison pills*. It was also a decade of considerable monkey business—*sleazebags* and *sleazeballs* engaging in *white-collar crime* and *insider trading*, often leaving *paper trails* that led to *smoking guns* and *white-collar prisons*.

As the decade rolled along, Boomer was bombarded with hundreds of *high-tech* brave new words for a brave new world of science and technology. She found herself playing *telephone tag* with such *cutting edge* dictionary entries as *blusher*, *bullet train*, *call forwarding* and *call waiting*, *cold fusion*, *faux pearls* (and *faux anything else*), *fuzz-buster*, *greenhouse effect* (coined in 1937, but really an '80s word, like *ozone depletion*), *makeover*, *meltdown*, *microwaveable*, *nuclear winter*, *SDI* and *Star Wars* (not just a movie anymore), *super collider*, *tanning booth* (and *bed*), *voice activated*, and *voice mail* (a new oxymoron). As the wonders of the computer *impacted* on her mind, she acquired a new *user-friendly* vocabulary: *desktop publishing*, *kludge*, *laptop*, *micro*, *number crunching*, and *spreadsheet*.

Boomer discovered a boom in the world of medicine: *arthroscopy*, *attention deficit disorder*, *bikini cut*, *genetic counseling*, *geriatrician*, *Ibuprofen*, *in vitro fertilization*, *liposuction*, *liquid diet*, *live liver donor transplant*, *Lyme disease*, *Minoxidil*, *passive smoking*, *PMS*, *product tampering*, *seasonal affective disorder* (which yields the bacronym SAD), and *toxic shock syndrome*. For a while, she joined the fitness craze and became a *triathlete* who built up her *glutes* with *low-impact aerobics*, *aquacise*, *dancercise*, and *jazzercise*.

At the same time, Boomer was troubled by the spread of *AIDS* (perhaps *the* word of the '80s) and drugs through the decade and the population—*ARC, AZT, HIV complex, homophobia,* and *safe sex* (had it ever been safe?); *crackhead, crackhouse, freebase, gateway drug, ice, narcoterrorism,* and *strip search.*

Our Boomer became swept up in a decade marked by considerable political and social change, and this change in turn left its mark on the American language—*action clothing, bag lady, build-down, codependent, condo conversion, Contra, coparent, designated driver, designer jeans* (*genes,* or anything else), *disinformation, exit poll, extended care, gentrification, gerontocracy, glasnost, gridlock, high top, Intifada, mall rat, no-growth, quality time, perestroika, POSSLQ, rust belt* (or *bowl*), *seatbelt laws, significant other, single parent, singles bar, stepfamily, superfund, surrogate mother,* and *wilding.*

During the '80s Boomer learned to come to terms with new entertainment terms, such as *boom box, breakdancing, bungee jumping, cable-ready, camcorder, clear channel, colorization, closed and open captioned, docudrama* and *documusical, ghetto blasters, hackysack, infotainment, MTV, new-wave music, new-age anything, slam dunk, snowboarding, sound bite, televangelist, veejay,* and *video, laser,* and *compact disks.*

Lucky Boomer. Throughout the '80s a growing interest by *foodies* in ethnic and regional cuisine added a menu of new words to the American palate and vocabulary—*bagel chips* and *bagel dogs, blush wine, brew decaf, callaloo, corn dogs, dim sum, enoki, fajita, frozen yogurt, green goddess dressing, ground turkey, oat bran, sea legs, shiitaki, surimi,* and *wine coolers.*

Boomer wasn't really distraught. She knew that, just as one never steps into the same river twice, one cannot step into the same language twice—that, even as one enters, the words are swept downstream into the future, forever making a different river. Or, to switch the metaphor, she knew that language is like a tree that sheds its leaves and grows new ones so that it may live on. Changes in our vocabulary occur not from decay or degeneration. Rather, new words, like new leaves, are essential to a living, healthy organism. A language draws its nutrients from the environment in which its speakers live. Throughout history, as people have met with new objects, experiences, and ideas, they have needed new words to describe them. During the 1980s, the tree of American English experienced a riot of new growth—a sign that our multifoliate language is deeply rooted in the nourishing soil of change.

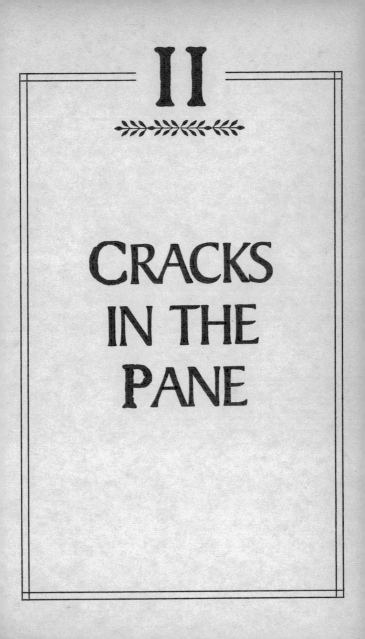

II

CRACKS IN THE PANE

IS ENGLISH
PREJUDICED?

So far, I have been singing the praises and praising the songs of language—"the human essence," "more to the mind than light is to the eye." But nothing that lives is perfect, including people and languages. We human beings are not computers that generate objective, bias-free, and mistakeproof words, phrases, and sentences. Our speech and our writing inevitably reflect the fearful asymmetry of our kind. In this chapter and the three that follow I shall identify some of the frets and the flaws and pitfalls and pratfalls of language in general and the English language in particular.

Language is a window through which we look at the world. A growing number of people have begun to wonder if our window on reality has a glass that distorts the view. If language reflects culture and in turn influences culture, could it be that the window through which we see life is marked by cracks, smudges, blind spots, and filters? In short, is language prejudiced?

To the estimated five percent of the population that is left-handed, many devices, from doorknobs to school desks, from athletic gear to musical instruments, from can openers to flush handles on toilets, seem to be made for right-handed people. What is even more insidious is that language itself may be designed for the right-handed majority.

Does language libel the left-handed? To discover the reputations that seemingly innocent words like *left* and *right* have in English, read the following sentences and ask yourself if the impression you receive is favorable or unfavorable:

- I believe that you are in the right about this issue.
- Her left hand doesn't know what the right hand is doing.
- Throckmorton is the boss's right-hand man.
- Melinda is certainly a dexterous and adroit athlete.
- The FBI has uncovered a sinister plot.
- Pringle is not only gauche in cocktail conversation but gawky on the dance floor. He was born with two left feet.
- When it comes to grammar, I feel out in left field.

Such statements reveal that *right* in English often suggests correctness, rectitude, and importance. Being right or on the right hand means being in the favorite position. Who ever heard of someone having a left-hand man?

Two words we use to praise skill are *dexterous*, which comes to us from the Latin *dexter*, meaning "right" or "right hand," and *adroit*, from the French *à droit*, "to the right." On the other hand (the left one, of course), *sinistra*, the Latin for "left hand," yields the uncomplimentary *sinister* in English. The French for "left hand" is *gauche*; in English it means "crude, lacking in social grace" and is debased in form to *gawky*, as contrasted to *dexterous* and *adroit*. Somehow, having two right feet is less gawky than having two left ones, and to be out in left field is to be way off base—a left-handed compliment at best.

Black Americans make up twelve percent of our population. Speaking for many black people, author and actor Ossie Davis contends that the English language is the black American's enemy: "Who speaks to me in my Mother Tongue damns me indeed! . . . the English language—in which I cannot conceive myself as a black man without, at the same time, debasing myself."

Under *black* in *The Random House Dictionary of the English Language* (1987) we find, among other meanings: "gloomy; pessimistic; dismal: *a black outlook*; deliberately harmful; inexcusable: *a black lie*; boding ill; sullen or hostile; threatening: *black words; black looks;* . . . without any moral quality or goodness; evil; wicked: *His black heart has concocted yet another black deed*; indicating censure, disgrace, or liability to punishment: *a black mark on one's record*; marked by disaster or misfortune: *black areas of drought; Black Friday;* . . . based on the grotesque, morbid, or unpleasant aspects of life: *black comedy; black humor;* . . . done or written in black to indicate, as on a list, that which is undesirable, substandard, potentially dangerous, etc.. *Pilots put a black flag next to the ten most dangerous airports*; illegal or underground: *The black economy pays no taxes;* . . . deliberately false or intentionally misleading: *black propaganda*."

In contrast, what do we find under *white* in the same unabridged dictionary?: "*Slang:* decent, honorable, or dependable: *That's very white of you*; auspicious or fortunate; morally pure, innocent; without malice; harmless: *white magic.*"

Is it true that in English *black* often conjures up the unsavory or (here's that word again) sinister, while *white* is often associated with things or ideas that are right? Ask yourself which of the following black and white expressions have a favorable, neutral, or unfavorable suggestion:

• black art, blackball, black belt, blackbird, black book, black cat, black coffee, black deed, black eye, blackface, black flag, Black Friday, blackguard, blackhearted, black hole, black humor, blackjack, black lie, blacklist, black look, black magic, blackmail, black mark, black market, black mass, black mood, blackout, black sheep, black tie, basic black, in the black

• white belt, white bread, white Christmas, whitecollar worker, white dwarf, white elephant, white flag, white-glove, white heat, White Knight, white lie, white of you, white magic, white meat, white nights, white noise, white slavery, whitewash, whitewall, white with rage, lily white

The black list contains only three expressions with positive suggestions—*black belt, black tie,* and *in the black* (can you think of any others in the English language? I can't), while at least half the items in the white list are favorable, suggesting fairness (*that's white of you*), professionalism (*white-collar worker, white-glove treatment*), harmlessness (*white magic, white lie*), purity (*lily white, white-glove, White Knight*), or peace (*white flag*). But what can you expect from a language in which white pastry is called *angel food cake* and dark pastry *devil's food cake*?

While left-handed and black people are minorities in the United States, women make up the majority of the population in almost every country in the world. Yet concern has been growing that the English language stigmatizes women as an inferior group of human beings, undermines their self-images, and restricts their perceptions of life's possibilities. As a way of examining this contention, I ask you to answer the following questions as precisely and honestly as you can and to compare your responses with the comments that come afterward.

1. In each pair, which term carries more respect: bachelor-spinster, master-mistress, sir-madam, poet-poetess, major-majorette, governor-governess?

The first word in each set carries more prestige than the second. *Spinster* began its life meaning simply "a woman who spins." Today *spinster* suggests a rejected, dried-up "old maid," so much so that some single women are driven to adopt the ludicrous labels *bachelorette* and *bachelor girl* to describe their status.

What about *master* and *mistress*, cognates formed from the same root? We can see the power and respect accorded *master* in such expressions as *master craftsman*, *Mastercard*, and *master of my fate*. *Mistress*, on the other hand, has taken on so much illicit sexual meaning that it has become an unusable, tongue-in-cheek dirty joke. The situation is much the same with *sir* and *madam*: *Sir* is unfailingly a term of respect, while *madam* has about it the whiff of the brothel manager. As feminist Gloria Steinem has asked, how would a man feel if he were graduated with a "spinster of arts degree"—or a "mistress of science degree," for that matter?

The other masculine forms in the first question also carry an added degree of power and excellence. *Poetess* suggests a quaint, drawing-room version of a poet, who writes only about bluebirds and sunsets. A majorette is a mere twirler of batons (certainly not a major activity), a governess governs only the romper room. In her successful bid for the Connecticut governorship, the late Ella Grasso had to contend with the opposition's slogan "Connecticut Doesn't Need a Governess."

Incidentally, the only common word-pair in English in which the male form derives from the female is *widow-widower*.

2. If a king rules a kingdom, what does a queen rule? If a man mans a station, what does a woman do? If a man fathers a movement, what does a woman do? If a man who pursues freewheeling relationships with women is a womanizer or a philanderer, what do we call a woman who plays the field of men?

Queens, of course, rule kingdoms, not "queendoms," and nobody "womans" a station or "mothers" a movement. Apparently we English speakers feel that nouns like *queendom* and verbs like *to woman* and *to mother* are too weak. But language can change. *To father* a child may mean little more than to provide the sperm necessary for birth, and *to mother* a child may mean more than we sometimes want it to. The rise of *to parent* in our language has given us just the androgynous word we need to express the coadventure of being a parent and to unite the two sexes in mutual activity.

The idea that a female can pursue men as sex objects is, apparently, so unthinkable that the only words we have for such a person are condemning: *tease, loose woman, easy mark, slut, nymphomaniac,* and *whore.*

3. What do you picture when you hear or read the following expressions: *The Ascent of Man, Renaissance Man, Language separates mankind from the other creatures, Everyone should guard his valuables?*

Do words like *man, mankind,* and *he* include women and children? This question was tested by sociologists who asked three hundred college students to select illustrations from pictures that were supplied for chapters in a textbook. One group of students was presented titles such as "Social Man," "Industrial Man," and "Political Man," the other, titles such as "Society," "Industrial Life," and "Politics." Results indicated that the word *man* evoked pictures of males participating in that activity far more than women or children. Another survey revealed that children from kindergarten through seventh grade interpreted the sentences "Man must work in order to eat" and "Around the world man is happy" to mean male adults, not females and children. How, we might ask, did all those Renaissance men manage to reproduce when we never hear about any Renaissance women?

In *Words and Women: New Language in New Times* (1979) Casey Miller and Kate Swift discuss the effect of *man* as the generic term. They note that we would not be surprised by the statement "Man is the only primate that commits rape," but we would be unlikely to pass without comment over the statement "Man, being a mammal, breast-feeds his young." In

English morphology, it appears, the male does *not* embrace the female.

Of our six types of pronouns—first-, second-, and third-person singular and plural—only one, the third-person singular, identifies the sex of the individual. Many languages avoid sexual designation in their pronouns, as in the Turkish, *o*, which can mean either *he* or *she*. Among the candidates proposed to displace the generic third-person singular pronoun in English are *co*, *et*, *han*, *hesh*, *jhe*, *na*, *person*, *s/he*, *thon*, *ti* (an inversion of the letters in *it*), and *ws*, but none has caught on.

Two centuries ago the plural pronoun was perfectly acceptable in sentences like "Everyone should guard their valuables." That shouldn't surprise you if you open yourself to the plurality of the pronoun *everyone*. Fill in the blank in the following sentence: "Everyone in the building attended the party, and _____ had a wonderful time." Most English speakers would supply a *they*. Why shouldn't the *everyone-they* pairing pass the same muster?

Today such a disagreement of number will set the teeth of the language purist agnashing, so I cannot recommend unrestricted commerce between *everyone* and *they*. The more judicious strategy is to make the entire statement plural, as in "All students [customers, etc.] should guard their valuables." In fact, once you set your mind to it, you will soon find it quite natural to use *humankind* in place of *mankind* and to replace *chairman* with the metonymous *chair*, a word, incidentally, that has been around in this sense for three centuries.

4. In each pair, which name forms the basis for

the other?: *Victor-Victoria, Paul-Paula-Pauline-Paulette, Henry-Henrietta.*

Although there are many exceptions, female names in our culture are often derivatives of male names, as in the examples above. In contrast, males are assigned strong, independent first names and retain their fathers' last names their whole lives. When names like *Marion, Shirley,* and *Beverley* come to be shared by both sexes, their use for males is generally discontinued.

5. Which of the following people are married and which are single: *Mr. John Smith, Mrs. John Smith, Miss Mary Jones, Ms. Gloria Steinem?*

Social custom announces the potential sexual availability of a woman by her name. Mr. John Smith may be married or single, but Mrs. John Smith is definitely married. In addition, she has acquired her husband's last name, passively defined in relationship to his identity. We who use such titles think they are ancient and proper. But they aren't. Miller and Smith write, "Martha Washington would have been mystified to receive a letter addressed to Mrs. George Washington. *Mrs.* was interchangeable with *Mistress* . . . and *Mistress George* would have made little sense." How many men would be willing to derive their first names from women's names? How many men would be willing to give up their last names in marriage?

Miss Mary Jones is, of course, unattached—and fair game, but Ms. Gloria Steinem, like Mr. John Smith, may be single or married. It is the unequal state of affairs that exists between *Mr. John Smith* and *Miss Mary Jones* that women are protesting when they ask to be identified as *Ms.* rather than *Mrs.* or *Miss,* or simply to be called *Mary Jones*. Centuries ago, *mistress* did not necessarily identify a woman as married or kept. *Mrs.* arose as an abbreviation of *mistress*, and *Miss* as a clipping of that word. Despite complaints that *Ms.* has about it an unattractive sound and that the letters look like the abbreviation of *manuscript*, *Ms.* is a sincere attempt to return to a connubially neutral designation for women that matches the one for men.

Read and hear this: "Whan that Aprill with his shoures soote/The droughte of March hath perced to the roote. . . ." These are the opening lines of Geoffrey Chaucer's *Canterbury Tales* in Middle English. The history of English, like that of all living languages and living things, is the history of constant change. I believe that our language can change so that men, women, and children can be free to imagine and explore the full range of their potential. We limit and diminish males and females alike when we use sexist language. In doing so, we become prisoners of language and abandon that which makes us human: the capacity to distinguish, discriminate, compare, and evaluate.

In 1953 the National Weather Service began conferring female first names on all hurricanes, categorizing those devastating winds as female. Twenty-six years later, the Service started identifying hurricanes by both male and female names alternately: Alma, Bertram, Charlotte, Donald, Elaine, and so on. That one small step for humankind demonstrates that we can control our language, that we are language inventors endowed with the capacity to create genuinely inclusive nouns and pronouns to refer to ourselves. We can stop identifying men as the norm and women as the aberrant, subordinate, or diminutive. We can invent words that transcend labeling women by marital status, and we can fashion descriptions like *flight attendant*, *letter carrier*, and *server* that avoid the lexical unfairness of stereotyping jobs by sex. As our language becomes more humane by becoming more truly human, we shall all—men, women, and children—feel better about ourselves and the world in which we live and move and have our being.

≫≫≫≫≫≪≪≪≪≪

WORDS WE NEED

*C*hoconivorous is "the tendency when eating a chocolate Easter bunny, to bite off the head first." The *hozone* is "the place where one sock in every laundry load disappears to." And a *charp* is "the green, mutant potato chip found in every bag."

Welcome to the world of sniglets, the series of pop dictionaries that attempt to describe the hitherto indescribable. Author (and actor-comedian) Rich Hall defines a sniglet as "any word that doesn't appear in a dictionary but should," which makes *sniglet* itself a sniglet. Hall's wiggy lexicons dazzle us with an inherent shortcoming of all vocabularies: No language has a net wide enough to throw over all of reality. There will always be more things and ideas than there are words.

At St. Paul's School I frequently ask my seniors to make up sniglets about our lives together in a boarding school community. As Rich Hall's sniglets books demonstrate again and again, granting something a name helps us to look at it through new eyes and to become more aware of its existence. I hope that, in the process of fabricating their own sniglets, my students will better understand the realities, dreams, fears, and joys of their lives at a residential school nestled in a valley in Concord, New Hampshire:

cryptocarnophobic (adj.) How one feels when mystery meat is placed on the table at evening seated meal.

gastro-optimize (v.) To go out to the cafeteria for more food in order to stay and talk with the ultimate scope. (In St. Paul's School slanguage a scope is a gorgeous member of the opposite sex.)

postpost (v.) To check your post office box five times a day even on Sunday when you know there can't be anything there.

SATarrhea (n.) The urge to go to the bathroom while taking the Scholastic Aptitude Test.

shmoffles (n.) The crud that accumulates on your cleats and falls off in the shape of waffles.

stud-ups (n.) The special kind of sit-ups executed by members of the football team while the field hockey team jogs by.

Blessed with the wealthiest vocabulary in the history of humankind, many English speakers feel that they have a word for everything. But, as the saga of sniglets illuminates, not even the English language can cast its net over all the things and ideas of life. As wondrously vast as our English vocabulary may be, there remain a surprisingly large number of concepts for which we still do not have good and serviceable words.

We have now embarked on a decade we call the

Nineties. With varying emotions, we look back on previous decades—the Twenties, Thirties, Forties, Fifties, Sixties, Seventies, and Eighties.

But after the Nineties, what? When the twenty-first century dawns, what are we going to call its first decade? The Zeros? Too dismal. The Noughts or Naughts? Too negative. The Aughts or Oughts? Too ambiguous, too prescriptive. Surely we can launch the next century with something more cheerful—perhaps the Ohs, an exultant exclamation that conveys the sense of wonder and infinite potential that awaits us.

And what about the decade after that, the one beginning with the year 2010?* The Teens leap to mind, but three of those years—2010, 2011, and 2012—will not include numbers in the teens.

When we reach the year 2020, we shall again be equipped with familiar decade names for the next eighty years, but the year 2026 will call out for another word we need but don't have. That year, of course, will mark the 250th anniversary of American independence. In 1876 we celebrated our centennial, in 1926 our sesquicentennial (from the Latin *sesqui* and English *centennial:* "one and a half hundred"), and in 1976 our bicentennial. What shall we call our 250th in 2026? When the town of Epsom, New Hampshire, attained

---

*Purists will fault me on these dates, pointing out that Christ was one year old at the end of the first year A.D. and that the first decade A.D. was not over until the end of the year 10. Each new decade, therefore, begins with the start of a year ending with the number one, not zero, and the second decade of the next century will begin with the year 2011, not 2010. These precise chronologists will stay home on the night of December 31, 1999, while we yahoos are dancing in the streets to celebrate the arrival of the new millennium. One year later, around midnight, the literalists will go out to ring in the twenty-first century and find only a small gathering of themselves.

its 250th year of incorporation in 1975, one of its leading citizens, Al Norris, invented the word *quatri-millennial*, literally "a quarter of a thousand." Perhaps our nation in 2026 will take its cue from Mr. Norris.

And what do we call ourselves as citizens of that nation? We say *Americans* and *the American people*, but an American identifies anyone in this hemisphere, from North to Central to South America, and the designation has historically rankled Latin Americans and Canadians. In *The American Language*, H. L. Mencken lists the many alternatives that have been proposed—*Unisians, Unitedstatesians, Columbards,* and the like—but none has earned a thumbs-up from the American people, or whatever it is we are.

Wanted: new ways to say it. New technologies create a variety of situations that become commonplace before the language, as vigorous as it is, can catch up. Many closures on coats, shirts, pants, skirts, and shoes are made of Velcro these days, yet we still talk about buttoning or zipping up our coats and lacing up our shoes. Many ice makers create frozen water in the form of orange slices. "I'd like two ice slices with my ginger ale," I request. "You mean ice cubes, don't you?" comes the reply. We cling to the old compound *ice cubes*, in the same way that we persist in talking about paper tablecloths, metal woods, green blackboards, and plastic silverware (and glasses of both the drinking and optical varieties)—but what's wrong with the rhyming *ice slices*?

We used to dial telephone numbers and dial up people and places. Now that most of us have converted from rotary to push-button phones, how do we make telephonic connections? Do we still dial them? We might continue to use the word, but dials are round and we are not really dialing. So we search for a verb that rings the bell (except that telephones no longer ring; they chirp) and is right on the button: "Sorry, I must have pushed the wrong number"; "I think I'll punch up Doris"; "I've got to index-finger the Internal Revenue Service"; *Press M for Murder*—all these verbs are too suggestive, aggressive, or absurd.

The English language includes a number of pronouns that denote both males and females—*I, me, you, we, us, they,* and *them*—but we lack embracive third-person-singular pronouns that also transcend gender bias. Faced with such a gap in our language, we concoct monstrosities like "Everyone put on his or her coat to keep himself or herself warm," or we try to make do with "Everyone put on their coat to keep themselves warm," and grammatical sensibilities are offended. In addition, most of us are bereft of a second-person-plural pronoun to use when we are addressing a group of people. Spanish speakers make such a distinction—*tu* (second-person singular, familiar), *vosotros* (second-person plural, familiar), *Usted* (second-person singular, polite), and *Ustedes* (second-person plural, polite)—and American southerners are lucky to have *you all* to use when talking to more than one person. Brooklyn-ites possess *youse* and *youse guys* and Western Pennsylvanians *younz* and *younz guys,* but I, as a New Englander who attempts to speak standard English, am barred from employing these useful pronouns.

Why is it that English often accumulates stockpiles of words to express negative concepts, but relatively few for positive ones? We have the verb *to stink,* but we don't have one that means "to smell fragrant." Sensing that the word *disabled* may be negative and exclusionary, the National Cristina Foundation recently offered a prize of $50,000 to the person who provided the most useful positive new word "that describes people with disabilities who are living productive, successful lives." The award went to B. Freer Freeman for his creation of "people with differing abilities," an expression that, in the words of the judges, "keeps people up front and emphasizes a spectrum of abilities." True, but, given its length, I must wonder if "people with differing abilities" will catch on.

Looking out for oneself can be a good and necessary thing to do. We need an affirmative word to describe such an attitude, yet all we have is the condemning adjective *selfish*. Although I don't care for the hyphen, I nominate *self-ful* for election to our vocabulary. I use it often at book signings, where I have noticed that men who wish to have a book inscribed and signed to them will confidently say, "Make it out to me!" while women are more likely to look uncomfortable and whisper apologetically, "You'll think this is terrible, but the book is just for me." I tell them that wanting a signed book for oneself is perfectly natural, a healthful and self-ful act.

Wanted: brave new words to express positive feelings and attitudes. Suppose you wish to communicate that you are feeling angry. You can, of course, trot out the standard adjectives *angry* and *mad*. But these are far from being your only choices. You can sneak up on the emotion with more subtle descriptors—*peeved*, *piqued*, *miffed*, and *put out*, or you can draw on *furious*, *outraged*, *boiling*, *berserk*, *rabid*, *infuriated*, *livid*, and *apoplectic* to paint a picture of your towering rage. You can throw in a dash of humor with slang—*sore*, *stung*, *steamed*, *riled*, *ripped*, *hacked*, *upset*, *ticked off, worked up, burnt up, hopping mad, in a stew, lost it, bent out of shape,* and *flying off the handle*—or you can opt for fancier, more dignified adjectives, such as *wrathful, acrimonious, exercised, irascible, vexed, provoked, rancorous, bilious,* and *incensed.*

Why is English festooned with so many words to express hostility but so few to express love? The ancient Greeks, vessels of sensibility that they were, had at least three. *Philia* signified the affectionate feelings that people have for their friends and close kin; *agape* represented the fondness that people harbored for their fellow human beings; *eros* was the name for passionate or sexual love.

We modern English speakers, vessels of insensibility that we sometimes are, have no such words with which to distinguish among the degrees and objects of our affections. Love may or may not conquer all, but the word *love,* like an all-purpose disinfectant, must do it all. We love our parents and children; we love our spouses and paramours. We love our country; we love country music. We love God; we love our new hat. We love *The Iliad;* we love *Love Story. Love* has become such a do-it-all convenience word that it debases the emotion that is so resonant with infinite variety. Perhaps that is why Tina Turner laments, "What's love got to do, got to do with it?/What's love but a second-hand emotion?" Perhaps that is why we find it so difficult to say to each other, "I love you."

Our confusion and squeamishness with *love* are reflected in a related problem of our times. For years it has been evident that we lack a good word to describe, much less introduce, the person of the opposite sex with whom one is living but to whom one is not married. "What's really needed," David Behrans of *Newsday* explains, "is one new word that will capture all the elements of blissful, unmarried cohabitation. The word must at least blend a reference to residency, a suggestion of sexuality, a shading of emotional care, a hint of permanence, and a dash, perhaps, of economic sharing." Our dictionaries cry out so loudly for such a precise word that tens of lexical candidates have rushed in to try to fill the gap. Few, if any, of these pretenders have earned a thumbs up.

Friend, boyfriend, girlfriend, and *companion* are too coy and too euphemistic to describe the relationship at issue and fail to identify the live-in arrangement. *Lover* (can't married folks be lovers, too?), *mistress,* and *paramour,* though fine, old words, do not convey that anybody is living with anybody else; on the contrary, they all have intimations of romantic secrecy. *Swain* and *consort* are too stuffy and medieval and apply only to males; *suitor* and *fiancé(e)* are just plain inaccurate. *Partner* sounds too commercial or clinical, while *cohabitor* is a mouthful that is cold and passionless. *Roommate* identifies the joint living arrangement but not the emotional arrangements, *significant other* suggests a close, sharing relationship but not necessarily the cohabitation, and *mate* calls to mind tossing seas or the jungle: "Me Tarzan, you Jane."

San Francisco Chronicle columnist Herb Caen has proposed the term *ummer* as the solution to the problem. Caen's suggestion arises from the very human resolution of the verbal dilemma facing a mother introducing her daughter's live-in partner of the opposite sex: "And this is Roger, my daughter's . . . um, er . . ." Clever, clever; ha, ha—but *ummer* is surely not an enduring word.

What, then, are we going to call people who used to be known as "living in sin"? The U.S. Census Bureau, which, like nature, abhors a vacuum, invented the term *POSSLQ* for the 1980 head count. *POSSLQ* (pronounced (PAH-sul-kyoo) is an acronym, the letters of which stand for "Persons of Opposite Sex Sharing Living Quarters." Typical of acronyms, it is totally devoid of romance, just as we might expect from a contrivance of the U.S. Census Bureau.

My candidate for the *bon mot* to describe the situation under discussion is *covivant*, which began appearing in the late 1970s. The word captures and coalesces the intimacy of *lover* and *significant other*, the cohabitual accuracy of *roommate* and *POSSLQ*, the sexual equality of *fiancé(e)* and *partner*, and the cutesy-poohness of *ummer*. Beverly McDonald, a Bow, New Hampshire, reader of my column, hints at these qualities in her wonderfully original poem:

If I could be your covivant,
I'd be so proud, I'd boast and vaunt,
Compose a rhyme, a sweet romaunt,
To you my gallant, bold gallánt:

Were you to be my covivant,
You'd never need a restaurant.
I'd feed you any food you'd want—
A shrimp fondue, a cheese croissant—
Cuisine to please a dilettante.
(At least you'd not be lean and gaunt.)

You'd be my fellow covivant:
My piquant, mellow occupant,
Not gallivant as you were wont,

A misbehaving miscreant,
With debutantes, their hair bouffant,
And painted faces by du Pont!

On holidays we'd take a jaunt
Away from parents, uncle, aunt.
Undaunted, we'd vamoose, avaunt
Up to the mountains of Vermont,
Repair there to some cozy haunt:
"Monsieur and Madam Coe Vivant."

You needn't be a wise savant
Nor buy me diamond rings to flaunt,
Nor be a slave or sycophant
To in-laws who might tease and taunt,
Just nonchalant, yet au courant—
We'd live the good life, bon vivant!

In *covivant* we may have the perfect solution to our problem. Fashioned from the Latin *co*, "together," and French *vivant*, "living," *covivant* is bilingually enduring and endearing. Its Latinateness communicates a sense of permanence and stability, and its Frenchness lends the perfume of romance. As we see in Beverly McDonald's verse, the word gains additional vibrancy by reminding us of the bubbly *bon vivant*.

Viva *covivant*!

THE DEPARTMENT OF REDUNDANCY DEPARTMENT

On the grounds of St. Paul's School, where I have taught English for almost three decades, stand two signs that announce, "Private Property: No Trespassing Without Permission." Early in my career at the school I explained to the administration that the warning was redundant, that by definition the act of trespassing is committed without permission. My suggestions that the last two words in the signs be painted out were met with polite smiles, but tradition endures and prevails in New England boarding schools. Now more than twenty-five years later, the signs still stand and so do their messages. Unauthorized visitors are still required to obtain permission before they trespass on our grounds.

I am surrounded by an army of recurrently repetitive redundancies. In fact, I am completely surrounded. Even more than that, I am completely surrounded on all sides. These repeated redundancies are in close proximity to my immediate vicinity, which is a lot worse than their being in distant proximity in a vicinity far away.

I turn on the radio or television and learn that "at 10 A.M. in the morning" a man has been found "fatally slain," "leaving no living survivors," that three convicts "have successfully escaped" (how else does one do it?), that "foreign imports" are threatening to destroy the balance of trade (by outnumbering the domestic imports, presumably), that the weather is "minus ten degrees below zero," and etc., etc.

Sports announcers inform me that a certain fullback has had his "forward progress stopped," that a promising young athlete "has a fine future ahead of him" (while my athletic future is long behind me), and that a track star has just set a "new record," a feat much more newsworthy than setting an old record.

I am adrift in a sea of American overspeak. The sea is a perfectly appropriate metaphor here, for the word *redundancy* is a combination of the Latin *undare*, "to overflow" and *re-*, "back," and literally means "to overflow again and again," which may itself be a bit redundant. It may come as an unexpected surprise (even more surprising than an expected surprise) that the ancient Greeks had a name for this rhetorical blunder—*pleonasmus*.

Richard Nixon eulogized the life of statesman Adlai Stevenson with these words: "In eloquence of expression he had no peers and few equals." Peers are not superiors; they *are* equals. When asked about his vice-presidential ambitions, Mayor Robert Wagner of New York said, "I have reiterated over and over again what I have said before." Other gems of political overspeak include "I'm in favor of letting the status

quo stay as it is," "I'm going to proceed ahead. Someone has to do it," and "In the 1930s we were not just a
nation on our backs. We were prone on our backs." I
assure you that none of these examples is a figment of
my imagination, or a figment of any other part of me.
They are all true facts.

The pervasive and persuasive messages of advertising are fraught with false pretenses, which are a lot
more dangerous than true pretenses. The hucksters
think they can treat us all like country bumpkins, even
us city bumpkins. One stack of products is "100 percent
pure," certainly more pristine than being fifty percent
pure. Other product boxes trumpet the arrival of a
"bold, new innovation," which sure beats any bold, old
innovation, that is "new and improved." (Can something really be both new *and* improved?)

McDonald's hamburger emporia boast of "Billions
and Billions Sold," and I wonder if billions and billions
is any more than mere billions. Appliance companies
keep flooding the market with hot-water heaters, even
though these machines are obviously made to heat cold
water. And Raid insecticide "kills bugs dead," which is
just the way they should be killed.

All this linguistic overkill reminds me of Vaughn
Monroe's hit song of the 1950s, "There, I've Said It
Again" and stirs within me not just a sensation, but
one singular sensation. "Save 40% off!" blares the
typical special-sale sign. A Tucson strip joint advertises
"Totally, totally nude! Live girls," much more enter-
taining than partially nude dead girls. Various hotels
promise "a honeymoon for two"—the old-fashioned
kind! Of all the adspeak that clogs my mailbox the
most repetitively redundant is "free gift." Sometimes
I am even offered a "complimentary free gift." I sigh

with relief, grateful that I won't have to pay for that gift.

My fellow colleagues and classmates, I am here to tell you the honest truth, not to be confused with the dishonest truth, about redundancies. My past experience, which is a lot more reliable than my present or future experience, tells me that overspeak will not go away. The past history of the pleonasm gives us but a small inkling (can an inkling ever be large?) of the pleonasms that will fill our future history. Embedded in the idea of experience and history is the past, yet we persist in talking about someone's past experience and past history. Plans and warnings, in contrast, are by definition futuristic, yet every day we hear about future plans, advance warnings, and forewarnings. This chronic and chronological confusion is exemplified by the pretentious prefix pre-, as in *preboard*, *preheat*, *pretest*, *preplan*, and *prerecord*. While I concede that boarding, testing, and heating may be two-stage processes, I don't see how preplanning and prerecording differ from planning and recording. I have even seen shows "prerecorded before a live audience," certainly preferable to prerecording before a dead audience.

I do not overexaggerate, much less exaggerate, when I say that, far and away, the one and only pleonasm I most hate with a passion (rather than calmly hating it) is "at this point in time." Either "at this point" or "at this time" will do just fine, and "now" is even better. "At this point in time" is the bureaucrat's way of spelling "now" by using seventeen letters. This atrocity elicits from this old geezer (I confess that I am no longer a young geezer) an audible (louder than an inaudible) groan, exacerbates all my aches and pains, and sets me not just to ranting or to raving, but to ranting and raving. I am not just bound or just determined but bound and determined to stamp out the last vestige, rather than the first vestige, of this classic example of logorrhea and declare it not just null or just void, but null and void. May we not only cease or desist using "at this point in time," may we cease and desist.

Speaking of "aches and pains," "ranting and raving," "bound and determined," "null and void," and "cease and desist," English is riddled with the double jeopardy of these insidious pairs. Sure, some of them that look like redundancies aren't. I know that in "kith and kin" *kin* are family and relatives while *kith* are friends and neighbors, that in "scrimp and save" *scrimp* means to be frugal while *save* means to put money away, that the *beck* in "beck and call" is a beckoning gesture while the *call* is a vocal command, that in "hue and cry" *hue* is a general clamor attending a robbery while *cry* is a specific statement such as "Stop thief!", and that the *bag* in "bag and baggage" was originally the property of an individual soldier while *baggage* was the collective property of the army. I'll even concede that in "bought and paid for" one can buy something without completely paying for it and that in "fair to middling," *middling* may be a notch above *fair*.

But over and above these few exceptions I do not, as I live and breathe, understand the whys and wherefores of many other various and sundry twosomes, in which the two halves (certainly not three or more halves) are for all intents and purposes one and the same and say the exact same thing. Caught betwixt and between such examples of linguistic conspicuous consumption, I shall not hem and haw or slip-slide. Just to pick and choose a few more examples, these hard-and-fast doublets are anything but fine and dandy, tip-top, well and good, hale and hearty, fair and just, and spick-and-span.

Redundancies are the junk food of our language. Alas and alack, when we gorge on the empty calories of pleonasms, we accumulate adipose tissue in the nooks and crannies of our linguistic waistline in dribs and drabs and bits and pieces—and I challenge you to tell me the differences between alas and alack, a nook and a cranny, a drib and a drab, and a bit and a piece. Indeed, in this day and age redundancies are multiplying by fits and starts and leaps and bounds. Rather than aiding and abetting these fattening snack-size doublets, let us find the ways and means to oppose them with all our vim and vigor and might and main. Lo and behold, perhaps one day they will be over and done with and we shall be free and clear of them.

The consensus of opinion is that many of these pleonasms grow from a lack of appreciation for the root meanings of words, the source from whence (which means "from from where") they come. Derived from the Latin *sensus*, meaning "opinion," and *con-*, "a collection," a consensus of opinion is a collection of opinion of opinion. Believe me, I know about these translingual redundancies. After all, I live right next door to Vermont. The citizens of that verdant patch of New England actually drive around with license plates proclaiming, "Vermont: Green Mountain State," which translates to "Green Mountain: The Green Mountain State," if you'll pardon my French. Other French misses show up on our menus—"roast beef with au jus" and "soup du jour of the day." Be sure to record these in your daily journal.

If you know your Middle English, Greek, Anglo-

French, Latin, Italian, Japanese, Malay, and Chinese (doesn't everybody?), you will avoid talking about time and tide (which are simply "time and time"), Greenwich Village ("Greenvillage Village"), an epileptic seizure ("a seizure seizure"), the hoi polloi ("the the people"), beautiful calligraphy ("beautiful beautiful writing"), correct orthography ("correct correct writing"), a bunch of grapes ("a bunch of a bunch of grapes"), a handwritten manuscript ("handwritten handwriting"), something that is very true ("truly true"), pizza pie ("pie pie"), a head honcho ("head head"), shrimp scampi ("shrimp shrimp"), rice paddy ("rice rice"), and the Gobi Desert ("the Desert Desert"). Anyone with even an elementary knowledge of Middle English and Dutch should know that *lukewarm*, from the Dutch *leuk* through the Middle English *louke*, meaning "tepid," translates to "warmwarm." Okay, go ahead and be luke about my criticisms.

Can we ever cure ourselves of our national addiction to fatty and fattening redundancies that ooze into our parlance anywhere and everywhere, over and over, and again and again? I believe that we can. As the old adage goes, "If at first you don't succeed, try, try again." Of course, by their very nature adages are old. That is how they get to be adages.

The sum total and end result (about as final as you can get) are that we can join together (more effective than joining apart) to fight the good fight against every single one of these redundancies. We can drive them from our house and home. We can bring them, in the words of many a flight attendant and police officer, to a complete stop, and we can kill them dead. That would be so incredible it would be unbelievable.

ONE WORD CAN CHANGE THE WORLD

Next to Archie Bunker, the most eminent modern mangler of the English vocabulary is Emily Litella, the not-ready-for-prime-time character created by Gilda Radner on *Saturday Night Live*. A lineal descendant of Mrs. Malaprop, Emily could never understand why people got so upset by violins on television. What was the big deal about Soviet jewelry? Why all the pitch and moment about endangered feces? Might we not be better off with a little less? Informed of her verbal faux pas, Miss Litella would inevitably shrug and sigh, "Oh, never mind." Although Emily's droll response always stirred up hurricanes of laughter from her audiences, there are times in our liaisons with language when mind we must.

The colas of the world have been shaken up explosively by translation. When Pepsi-Cola tried to convert the slogan "Come alive with the Pepsi generation" into Chinese and German, the effort fizzled. In Chinese the message emerged as "Pepsi brings back your dead ancestors," in German as "Come out of the grave with Pepsi." The recent lifting of trade barriers with China allowed the rest of the world to discover what before had been the secret of a few wordwise students of Asian languages—that the name *Coca-Cola* in Chinese means "bite the wax tadpole." When General Motors introduced its Chevy Nova to Spanish-speaking countries, the campaign got off on a flat tire because *no va* in Spanish means "doesn't go."

One letter in error can mutate meaning beyond recognition. The administrators of the San Jose Public Library were forced to pull down a $10,000 banner because of a single vowel. The thirty-foot-high sign extended greetings to patrons in twenty-seven languages. A security guard who was a native of the Philippines noticed that the greeting of welcome in Tagalog, the national language of his islands, was marred by an unwittingly suggestive typo. The message should have read *tuloy po kayo* but the *o* in *tuloy* was inadvertently replaced by an *e*. That change was enough to alter the meaning from "welcome" to "circumcision."

A more serious mistake occurred when, in the early 1920s, two successive New Jersey legislatures passed an amendment providing that members of the General Assembly should be elected biannually. In 1925 the legislature was shocked to discover that *biannually* meant "twice a year," instead of "every two years." *Biennially* was the word the lawmakers should have used, but, for a full year, they were powerless to correct the error. Although the inconvenience to politicians, election officials, and voters cost taxpayers money and reddened the faces of legislators, the results were far from life-threatening. Not so in all cases of misspoken and miswritten language.

The Crimean War pitted the combined might of Great Britain, France, Turkey, and Sardinia against Russia. At stake was, ostensibly, control of the holy places of Jerusalem and, more obliquely, the strategic importance of the Crimean peninsula to the commerce and politics of the Black Sea area.

In 1854, the second year of the war, the allied forces captured the town of Balaklava. The Russians marshaled a large force eight miles to the northwest with the intent of reclaiming the port, but the attempt was unsuccessful and both sides suffered devastating casualties. The heaviest British losses were the result of a futile attack by the six hundred seventy men of a gallant light cavalry unit. The travesty and tragedy are immortalized by Alfred, Lord Tennyson in his poem "The Charge of the Light Brigade":

> Half a league, half a league,
> Half a league onward,
> All in the valley of Death,
>   Rode the six hundred.
> "Forward, the Light Brigade!
> Charge for the guns!" he said:
> Into the valley of Death
>   Rode the six hundred.
>
> "Forward the Light Brigade!"
> Was there a man dismayed?
> Not though the soldiers knew
>   Someone had blundered.
> Theirs not to make reply,
> Theirs not to reason why,
> Theirs but to do and die;—
> Into the valley of Death
>   Rode the six hundred.

"Someone had blundered." The nature of the blunder was a confusion about one word that meant one thing to the speaker but another to the receivers of his words. Fitzroy James Henry Somerset, Lord Raglan, commander of the British forces, gave the order to "charge the guns!" The "guns" to which he referred were an isolated battery over a slight rise in the valley and in plain sight from his vantage point. The only guns visible to James Thomas Brudnell, Earl of Cardigan and leader of the Light Brigade, were those of the tightly secured Russian battalion at the far end of the valley. The command seemed utter madness, but it was a command; while Raglan and his staff watched from behind the lines, Lord Cardigan dutifully led the charge into the Valley of Death. More than two-thirds of his men were killed or wounded.

That such a failure to communicate could result in the deaths of hundreds of soldiers is appalling, but there is evidence that World War II was extended by a deadly three weeks because of a single error in translation.

Victory in Europe came on May 8, 1945, and Japanese resistance on the island of Okinawa ended seven weeks later. On July 26, 1945, Churchill, Truman, and Stalin issued the Potsdam Declaration: Japan had to surrender unconditionally or accept the consequences.

The Japanese cabinet seemed to favor a settlement but had to overcome two major obstacles to compliance—the tenacity of the Japanese generals and the pride of the citizens of Japan. Needing time, the Imperial Cabinet issued a statement explaining that they were giving the peace offer *mokusatsu*.

Mokusatsu can mean either "We are considering it" or "We are ignoring it." Most Japanese understood that the reply to the surrender ultimatum contained the first meaning, but there was one notable exception. The man who prepared the English language translation of the statement for the Domei news agency used "ignore" in the broadcast monitored by the English-speaking press. To lose face by retracting the news release was unthinkable to the proud Japanese. They let the statement stand.

Believing that their proposal had been ignored or rejected and unaware that the Japanese were still considering the ultimatum, the Allies proceeded to open the atomic age. On July 28, 1945, American newspapers printed stories reporting that the Japanese had ignored the peace offer, and on August 6 President Harry Truman ordered an atomic bomb dropped on Hiroshima. A new era in human history was irretrievably begun.

The destructive power of the bomb was an emblem of the destructive potential of language misused and misunderstood. The dead and missing from the bombing of Hiroshima numbered 92,000. Another 42,000 victims were claimed three days later by the blast at Nagasaki. Concurrently, Russia declared war on Japan and invaded Manchuria.

In the twenty days that followed the confusion about *mokusatsu* more than 150,000 men, women, and children were lost. One word misinterpreted.

III

THE
LOOM
OF
LITERATURE

LITERARY
WORDMAKERS

Year after year, decade after decade, and century after century, new words spring from the human imagination and enter our collective consciousness. At the risk of offering a penetrating glimpse into the obvious, I would point out that these new words, neologisms as they are called, do not fall from the sky or turn up under trees or rocks. Language is invented, not discovered. When we think about inventions, we usually think of creations like the wheel, the electric light, and the automobile—things that humankind has not always possessed. Words are such an integral part of our consciousness that we believe they have always existed, like stones and grass and bushes. But this belief is not true. Like flint tools and weaving, each new word is inventively spoken or written for the very first time by a particular human being at a particular moment.

Although the identities of most word progenitors are hidden away in the attic of history, the creators of a number of neologisms can be identified. Not surprisingly, many of these wordmakers are novelists, poets, playwrights, and essayists who are gifted with a keen ear for language, who love to play with words, and who record their fanciful fabrications in print. Many of these literary artists are Dr. Frankensteins, in the best sense of that label, stitching together meaning-bearing elements called morphemes into something new and alive.

The etymological meaning of *poet* is "maker," and in a very literal sense some of the mightiest of English poets have been the makers of our vocabulary. The first great poet to write in English was Geoffrey Chaucer, who contributed many nouns that end with the French suffix *-tion*, including *attention, duration, fraction*, and *position*. Edmund Spenser, Chaucer's successor in the imperial line of British epic poets, was the first English writer who self-consciously cobbled new words. From Spenser's allegorical epic, *The Faerie Queene*, issue *blatant* and *braggadocio*, and he also bequeathed us *briny, shiny*, and *violin*. Joining Chaucer and Spenser in the pantheon of epic poets is John Milton. For his lofty and sonorous *Paradise Lost*, Milton needed a name for the hall of the fallen angels. Following the analogy of *pantheon*, Milton welded together *pan*, "all," and *demon*, "devil," to forge *pandemonium*, which literally means "a place of all demons." Because Satan and his company were noisy and mischief-making, the meaning of *pandemonium* has broadened to mean "uproar or tumult." Milton's noble and prolific mind also gave birth to *all-conquering, dimensionless, earthshaking, impassive, infinitude, lovelorn, sensuous*, and *smooth shaven*, as well as the expression *light fantastic*.

This process of literary neologizing has continued unstinted into our times. The working title for Joseph

Heller's modern classic novel about the mindlessness of war was *Catch-18*, a reference to a military regulation that keeps the pilots in the story flying one suicidal mission after another. The only way to be excused from flying such missions is to be declared insane, but asking to be excused is proof of a rational mind and bars excuse.

Shortly before the appearance of Heller's book in 1961, Leon Uris's *Mila 18* was published. To avoid confusion with the title of Uris's war novel, Heller and his editor decided to change *Catch-18* to *Catch-22*. The choice turned out to be both fortunate and fortuitous as the 22 more rhythmically and symbolically captures the double duplicity of both the military regulation itself and the bizarre world that Heller shapes in the novel. ("That's some catch, that Catch-22," observes Yossarian. "It's the best there is," Doc Daneeka agrees.) During the three decades since its literary birth, *catch-22*, generally lowercased, has come to mean any predicament in which we are caught coming and going and in which the very nature of the problem denies and defies its solution. So succinctly does *catch-22* embody the push-me-pull-you absurdity of modern life that the word has become the most frequently employed allusion in all of American literature.

Spanning more than four centuries, here is a panorama of men and women of letters matched with their verbal offspring and the known birthyears of their creations:

Sir Thomas More	*utopia*	1516
William Tyndale	*scapegoat*	1530
Sir Thomas Elyot	*irritate*	1531
Ben Jonson	*diary*	1581

William Shakespeare	*changeful*	1606
Francis Bacon	*placid*	1626
Sir Thomas Browne	*hallucination*	1629
John Dryden	*witticism*	1677
John Locke	*billion*	1690
Alexander Pope	*anticlimax*	1710
Colley Cibber	*flirtatious*	1718
Jonathan Swift	*yahoo*	1726
Lord Chesterfield	*etiquette*	1750
Horace Walpole	*serendipity*	1754
Samuel Foote	*ugh*	1765
Oliver Goldsmith	*cantankerous*	1773
Richard Brinsley Sheridan	*deadlock*	1779
Samuel Johnson	*fiddlededee*	1784
Samuel Taylor Coleridge	*intensify*	1817
George Gordon, Lord Byron	*blasé*	1819
Washington Irving	*almighty dollar*	1836
Thomas Carlyle	*decadent*	1837
Harriet Beecher Stowe	*underground railway*	1852
Artemus Ward	*galoot*	1866
Robert Browning	*artistry*	1868
Lewis Carroll	*chortle*	1872
Herman Melville	*Americana*	1886
Finley Peter Dunne	*southpaw*	1891
Mark Twain	*gossip column*	1893
George Ade	*panhandler*	1899
George Bernard Shaw	*superman*	1903
T. A. Dorgan	*hot dog*	1903
O. Henry	*side-kick*	1904
Gelett Burgess	*blurb*	1907
Willa Cather	*stuffed shirt*	1913

Ezra Pound	*alley cat*	1914
Henry James	*ivory tower*	1917
Karel Capek	*robot*	1921
Sinclair Lewis	*belittle*	1922
William Woodward	*debunk*	1923
H. L. Mencken	*Bible belt*	1925
Carl Sandburg	*honky-tonk*	1927
John Steinbeck	*Okie*	1939
John O'Hara	*moola*	1939
James Bertram	*honcho*	1947
Stephen Potter	*gamesmanship*	1947
Dr. Seuss	*nerd*	1950

In the next seven chapters, beginning with an English playwright whose works began to grace our lives just about four centuries ago, we shall explore in greater detail the contributions of those especially productive literary artists who, sculpting significance from air, have changed the world by changing the word.

A MAN OF FIRE-NEW WORDS

What do these three sentences have in common?:

Has Will a peer, I ask me.
I swear he's like a lamp.
We all make his praise.

Each is an anagram that uses all the letters in the name William Shakespeare, and each captures a luminous truth: Peerless Will Shakespeare shines through the centuries and inspires our praise.

Little information about William Shakespeare's personal life is available, but from municipal records we can deduce that he was born in the English village of Stratford-upon-Avon, in the county of Warwickshire, on April 23, 1564, and that after retiring to his hometown around 1611, he died there on April 23, 1616. Shakespeare's plays, which he wrote in London between approximately 1590 and 1613, have been in almost constant production since their creation. Because the playwright dealt with universal truths and conflicts in human nature, his tragedies, comedies, and history plays continue to draw audiences from all walks of life, just as they did in their own day. Time has proven the truth of what Shakespeare's contemporary, Ben Jonson, said of him: "He was not of an age, but for all time."

An often neglected aspect of William Shakespeare's genius is that his words, as well as his works, were not just of an age, but for all time. He was, quite simply, the greatest wordmaker who ever lived. Ongoing research demonstrates that there are 20,138 lemmata (dictionary headwords) in Shakespeare's published works. That figure represents approximately forty percent of the total recorded for the English language up to the year 1623—and Shakespeare could not have owned any dictionary in which he could have looked up these words! For purposes of comparison bear in mind that the written vocabulary of Homer totals approximately nine thousand words, of the King James Bible eight thousand, and of Milton ten thousand.

Of the 20,138 basewords that Shakespeare employs in his plays, sonnets, and other poems, his is the first known use of over 1,700 of them. The most verbally innovative of our authors and our all-time champion neologizer, Shakespeare made up more than 8.5 percent of his written vocabulary. Reading his works is like witnessing the birth of language itself.

"I pitied thee,/Took pains to make thee speak," says Prospero to Caliban in *The Tempest*. "I endow'd thy purposes/With words that made them known." Shakespeare is our Prospero; he dressed our thoughts with words and teemed our tongue with phrases. With-

out him, our "native English" would be, as Thomas
Mowbray says in *Richard II*:

> . . . an unstringed viol or a harp,
> Or like a cunning instrument cas'd up—
> Or being open, put into his hands
> That knows no touch to tune the harmony.

Consider the following list of fifty representative
words that, as far as we can tell, Shakespeare is the first
to use in writing. So great is his influence on his native
tongue that we find it hard to imagine a time when
these words did not exist:

accommodation	dwindle	monumental
aerial	eventful	multitudinous
amazement	exposure	obscene
apostrophe	fitful	pedant
assassination	frugal	perusal
auspicious	generous	pious
baseless	gloomy	premeditated
bedroom	gnarled	radiance
bump	hurry	reliance
castigate	impartial	road
clangor	indistinguishable	sanctimonious
countless	invulnerable	seamy
courtship	lapse	sneak
critic (and critical)	laughable	sportive
dexterously	lonely	submerge
dishearten	majestic	useless
dislocate	misplaced	

Now add to these individual words Shakespeare's
daring originality with compounds. He created such
splendid audacities as *proud-pied April*, *heaven-kissing
hill*, and *world-without-end hour*, and he bequeathed
the English language such now-familiar double plays

as *barefaced, civil tongue, cold comfort, eyesore, faint-hearted, fancy free, foregone conclusion, foul play* (and *fair play*), *green-eyed, half-cocked, heartsick, high time, hotblooded, itching palm, lackluster, laughing-stock, leapfrog, lie low, long-haired, love affair, ministering angel, pitched battle, primrose path, sea change, short shrift, snow-white, stony-hearted, tongue-tied, towering passion,* and *yeoman's service.* The striking compound that Shakespeare fashioned to describe Don Adriano de Armando in *Love's Labour's Lost* is an appropriate epithet for the playwright himself: "a man of fire-new words."

Oscar Wilde once quipped, "Now we sit through Shakespeare in order to recognize the quotations." Unrivaled in so many other ways in matters verbal, Shakespeare is unequaled as a phrasemaker. "All for one, one for all," and "not a creature was stirring, not even a mouse," wrote Alexandre Dumas in *The Three Musketeers* and Clement Clark Moore in *The Night Before Christmas*. But Shakespeare said them first— "One for all, or all for one we gage" in *The Rape of Lucrece* and "not a mouse stirring" in *Hamlet*.

A student who attended a performance of *Hamlet* came away complaining that the play "was nothing more than a bunch of clichés." The reason for this common reaction is that so many of the memorable expressions in *Hamlet* have become proverbial. In that one play alone were born *brevity is the soul of wit, there's the rub, to thine own self be true, it smells to heaven, the very witching time of night, the primrose path, though this be madness, yet there is method in it, dog will have his day, the apparel oft proclaims the man, neither a borrower nor a lender be, frailty, thy name is woman, something is rotten in the state of*

Denmark, more honored in the breach than the observance, hoist with his own petard, the lady doth protest too much, to be or not to be, sweets for the sweet, to the manner born, and *more in sorrow than in anger.*

Cudgel your brain, and you can append a sample of everyday, idiomatic phrases from other Shakespearean plays: If you knit your brow and wish that this disquisition would vanish into thin air because it is Greek to you, you are quoting William Shakespeare in all his infinite variety. If you point the finger at strange bedfellows and blinking idiots, you are converting Shakespeare's coinages into currency. If you have seen better days in your salad days, when you wore your heart on your sleeve, you are, whether you know it or not, going from Bard to verse. If you break the ice with one fell swoop, if you never stand on ceremonies, play it fast and loose until the crack of doom, paint the lily, hope for a plague on both houses, are more sinned against than sinning because you have been eaten out of house and home by your own flesh and blood (the most unkindest cut of all), if you haven't slept a wink and are breathing your last because you're in a pickle, if you carry within you the milk of human kindness and a heart of gold (even though you know that all that glisters is not gold), laugh yourself into stitches at too much of a good thing, make a virtue of necessity, know that the course of true love never did run smooth, and if you won't budge an inch—why, if the truth be told and the truth will out, what the dickens, in a word, right on!, be that as it may, the game is up—you are, as luck would have it, standing on that tower of strength, that be-all and end-all of phrasemakers, William Shakespeare.

Shakespeare lurks in the most astonishing places. Some assert that the Porter's speech in act 2, scene 3 of

Macbeth is the source of the modern knock-knock joke: "Knock, knock, knock. Who's there i' th' name of Beelzebob? . . . Knock, knock. Who's there in th' other devil's name? . . . Knock, knock, knock. Who's there? Never at quiet!" And, if you look hard, you can find Shakespeare peeking out even from the pages of the Bible.

The most famous of all biblical translations is the King James Version, the brainchild of James I, who fancied himself a scholar and theologian. The king decided to assure his immortality by sponsoring a new Bible worthy of the splendor of his kingdom. To this end, James appointed a commission of fifty-four learned clerical and lay scholars, divided into three groups in Cambridge, Westminster, and Oxford. Three years of loving labor, 1608–1611, produced what John Livingston Lowes called "the noblest monument of English prose." Few readers would dissent from that verdict.

Among the many wonders of the King James Bible is that it stands as one of the few great accomplishments achieved by a committee. At the same time, some commentators have wondered why William Shakespeare was apparently not included among the fifty-four translators chosen. After all, Shakespeare had already written *Macbeth* in honor of King James (who also fancied himself an expert on witchcraft), and what better committee member could one ask for than the greatest poet of his age to work with the greatest collection of religious literature of all ages?

But an intriguing peculiarity in the King James Bible indicates that Shakespeare was *not* entirely absent from the monumental project. No one knows who made the astonishing discovery or how on earth he or she did it.

In 1610, the year of the most intensive work on

the translation, Shakespeare was forty-six years old. Given this clue, we turn to the forty-sixth psalm as it appears in the King James Bible. Count down to the forty-sixth word from the beginning and then count up to the forty-sixth word from the end, excluding the cadential *Selah*:

> God is our refuge and strength, a very present help in
> trouble.
> Therefore will not we fear, though the earth be
> removed,
> and though the mountains be carried into the midst
> of the sea;
> Though the waters thereof roar and be troubled,
> though the mountains shake with the swelling
> thereof. Selah.
> There is a river, the streams whereof shall make glad
> the city of God,
> the holy place of the tabernacle of the Most High.
> God is in the midst of her; she shall not be moved:
> God shall help her, and that right early.
> The heathen raged, the kingdoms were moved:
> he uttered his voice, the earth melted.
> The Lord of hosts is with us; the God of Jacob is our
> refuge. Selah.
> Come, behold the works of the Lord,
> what desolations he hath made on earth;
> He maketh wars to cease unto the end of the earth;
> he breaketh the bow, and cutteth the spear in
> sunder;
> he burneth the chariot in the fire.
> Be still, and know that I am God:
> I will be exalted among the heathen, I will be
> exalted in the earth.

The Lord of hosts is with us; the God of Jacob is our
  refuge. Selah.

If you counted accurately, your finger eventually
lit upon the two words *shake* and *spear*. Shakespeare.
Whether or not he created the majesty of the forty-
sixth psalm, he is in it. Whether the embedded *shake
spear* is a purposeful plant or the product of happy
chance, the name of the world's most famous poet
reposes cunningly in the text of the world's most
famous translation.

Shakespeare also hides in many works of twentieth-century literature. He was a busy and prolific
writer who, in twenty-five years, turned out thirty-
seven long plays and coauthored several others, yet he
still found time to provide titles for their books to
generations of authors who return again and again to
the well of his felicitous phrasing.

Take *Macbeth*, for example. Near the end of the
play, Macbeth expresses his darkening vision of life:
"It is a tale/Told by an idiot, full of sound and fury,/
Signifying nothing." Centuries later, William Faulkner
purloined a phrase from that speech for his novel *The
Sound and the Fury*, which is indeed told by an idiot,
Benjy Compson. Earlier in the play one of the witches
chants, "By the pricking of my thumbs,/Something
wicked this way comes." Agatha Christie plucked the
first line and Ray Bradbury the second as titles of their
bestsellers. Other steals from just the one play, *Macbeth*, include Robert Frost's "Out, Out—," Rose Macauley's *Told by an Idiot*, Ellis Middleton's *Vaulting
Ambition*, Adrienne Rich's *Of Woman Born*, Ngaio
Marsh's *Light Thickens*, Anne Sexton's *All My Pretty
Ones*, Allistair MacLean's *The Way to Dusty Death*,

Edward G. Robinson's *All Our Yesterdays*, Philip Barry's *Tomorrow and Tomorrow*, Malcolm Evans's *Signifying Nothing*, and John Steinbeck's *The Moon Is Down*.

From three other high school favorites—*Julius Caesar*, *Hamlet*, and *Romeo and Juliet*—have been lifted the titles of Robert Stone's *The Dogs of War*, James Barrie's *Dear Brutus*, John Gunther's *Taken at the Flood*, Barry Sadler's *Cry Havoc*, R. Lance Hill's *The Evil That Men Do*, Thornton Wilder's *The Ides of March*, H. Hall's *The Valiant*, David Halberstam's *Noblest Roman*, A. G. MacDonnell's *How Like an Angel*, Rex Stout's *How Like a God*, Joyce Martins's *Rosemary for Remembrance*, Arthur Schnitzler's *Undiscovered Country*, Ernest Hebert's *A Little More Than Kin*, Robert B. Parker's *Perchance to Dream*, Edith Wharton's *The Glimpses of the Moon*, Philip K. Dick's *Time Out of Joint*, Richard Yates's *A Special Providence*, Ogden Nash's *The Primrose Path*, Frederic Manning's *Her Privates, We*, Eric Knight's *This Above All*, Tom Stoppard's *Rosencrantz and Guildenstern Are Dead*, Louis Auchincloss's *The Indifferent Children*, Maxwell Anderson's *Both Your Houses*, Dorothy Parker's *Not So Deep as a Well*, Ford Madox Ford's *It Was the Nightingale*, Frederick Reynolds's *Fortune's Fool*, and Henry Wade's *No Friendly Drop*.

Add to these Aldous Huxley's *Brave New World*, James Stewart Carter's *Full Fathom Five*, Ellen Glasgow's *Barren Ground*, and Andrew Soutar's *Strange Bedfellows* (all from *The Tempest*); Faye Kellerman's *The Quality of Mercy* and S. N. Behrmann's *Rain from Heaven* (*The Merchant of Venice*); W. Somerset Maugham's *Cakes and Ale* (*Twelfth Night*), John Steinbeck's *The Winter of Our Discontent* (*Richard III*), Louis D'Alton's *Lovers' Meeting* (*Twelfth Night*) Gregory Mcdonald's *Merely Players* (*As You Like It*), John van Druten's *Bell, Book, and Candle* (*King John*), Richard Oke's *Wanton Boys* (*King Lear*), Noël Coward's *Pomp and Circumstance* (*Othello*), Frank Swinnerton's *The Merry Heart* (*Much Ado About Nothing*), Robert Herrick's *The Web of Life* (*All's Well That Ends Well*), Dorothy Reynolds's *Salad Days* (*Antony and Cleopatra*), Upton Sinclair's *A Giant's Strength* (*Measure for Measure*), Robert Penn Warren's *At Heaven's Gate* (*Cymbeline*), and Francis Ferguson's *Naked to Mine Enemies* (*Henry VIII*), Benjamin Webster's *One Touch of Nature* (*Troilus & Cressida*), and Vladimir Nabokov's *Pale Fire* (*Timon of Athens*); and from the sonnets, John Herbert's *Fortune and Men's Eyes*, Gary Wills's *Bare Ruined Choirs*, Marcel Proust's *Remembrance of Things Past* (the English translation, of course), Malcolm Muggeridge's *Chronicles of Wasted Time*, W. H. Auden's *The Dyer's Hand*, and Anthony Burgess's *Nothing Like the Sun* (a romantic novel about Shakespeare himself)—and it becomes evident that William Shakespeare was one of the most generous souls who ever set quill to parchment. Although he himself was never granted a title, he freely granted titles to others.

The etymologist Ernest Weekley said of Shakespeare, "His contribution to our phraseology is ten times greater than that of any writer to any language in the history of the world." The critic Walter Pater exclaimed, "What a garden of words!" In sonnet CXVI the Bard himself wrote, "If this be error and upon me proved,/I never writ, nor no man ever loved." If Shakespeare had not lived and written with such a loving ear for the music of our language, our English tongue would be immeasurably the poorer. No day goes by that we do not speak and hear and read and write his legacy.

NO HARMLESS
DRUDGES, THEY

He was, according to his biographer James Boswell, a huge man. When he was barely out of infancy, he contracted scrofula, a disease that severely impaired his eyesight and left his face horribly disfigured. He attended Oxford University but, because of family finances, did not take a degree. For a while he operated a private school, but that failed.

Yet on April 15, 1755, Samuel Johnson—fat, ugly, blind in one eye, and incompletely educated—produced the first modern *Dictionary of the English Language*. "Languages are the pedigrees of nations," he proclaimed, and, in compiling his wordbook, Johnson conferred a pedigree on the English-speaking nations. In garnering the rich, exuberant vocabulary of eighteenth-century England, the *Dictionary of the English Language* marks a turning point in the history of our tongue.

There had, of course, been earlier English dictionaries, the first being one Robert Cawdray's *A Table*

Alphabeticall, compiled, as he described it, for "ladies . . . or any other unskilfull persons." Published in 1604 and consisting of but one hundred twenty pages and just three thousand words, *A Table Alphabeticall* had as its purpose, as did the other dictionaries that appeared during the seventeenth century, the treatment of only the hardest and most scholarly words in our vocabulary.

Johnson set himself the task of making a different kind of dictionary, one that would include all the words in the English language, not just the difficult ones. In addition, he would show how to divide words into syllables and where words came from. He would establish a consistent system of defining words and draw from his own gigantic learning to provide, for the first time in any dictionary, illustrative quotations from famous writers. Johnson's lexicon, like its modern descendants, is a report on the way writers actually used the English language.

When a friend of his pointed out that it had taken forty French scholars forty years to accomplish what he proposed to do in three, Johnson replied, "Let me see: forty times forty is sixteen hundred. As three is to sixteen hundred, so is the proportion of an Englishman to a Frenchman."

And what an Englishman! Johnson, underfunded and working almost alone in a Fleet Street garret room, defined some 43,000 words and illuminated their meanings with more than 114,000 supporting quotations drawn from every area of literature. The task took nearer nine than three years, but the results more than justified Johnson's ambitious hopes. He captured the majesty of the English language and gave it a dignity that was long overdue. The two huge tomes, each the size of a lectern Bible and each of which would fill about five fat volumes today, were an immediate success upon their publication.

Johnson's friend and student, the actor David Garrick, composed a couplet comparing Johnson's single-handed labors with the collaborative product of the Académie Française:

> And Johnson, well arm'd like a hero of yore,
> Has beat forty French, and will beat forty more.

Johnson defined a lexicographer as "a writer of dictionaries, a harmless drudge that busies himself in tracing the original and detailing the signification of words." But he was obviously far more than a harmless drudge, and his dictionary was by far the most comprehensive and readable that had appeared. The reputation of the *Dictionary of the English Language* was so great that it dominated the field until the turn of this century and established a mighty line of thorough and scholarly English dictionaries that simply is not approached by those in any other language.

Dr. Johnson loved to use big words, and parts of his lexicon look forbiddingly convoluted and sesquipedalian to the modern-day reader:

cough. A convulsion of the lungs, vellicated by some sharp seriosity.

key. An instrument formed with cavities correspondent to the wards of a lock.

itch. A cutaneous disease extremely contagious,

which overspreads the body with small pustules filled with a thin serum.

network. Any thing reticulated or decussated, at equal distances, with interstices between intersections.

saw. A denated instrument, by the attrition of which wood or metal is cut.

Johnson was an eccentric man, and he saw no reason why he should keep his eccentricities and strong opinions out of his dictionary. Thus, many of his definitions are as much revelations of the author's personality as attempts to record the English language:

dedication. A servile address to a patron.

excise. A hateful tax levied upon commodities, and adjudged not by the common judges of property, but wretches hired by those to whom excise is paid.

gambler. (A cant word, I suppose for *game*, or *gamester*.) A knave whose practice it is to invite the unwary to game and cheat them.

goat. A ruminant animal that seems a middle species between deer and sheep.

lunch, luncheon. As much food as one's hand can hold.

oats. A grain, which in England is generally given to horses, but in Scotland supports the people.

opera. An exotic and irrational entertainment.

parasite. One that frequents rich tables, and earns his welcome by flattery.

patron. One who supports with insolence, and is paid with flattery.

pensioner. A slave of state hired by a stipend to obey his master. In England it is generally understood to mean pay given to a state hireling for treason to his country. [This definition became a sharp weapon in the hands of Johnson's enemies when he himself accepted a pension from George III.]

Tory. One who adheres to the ancient constitution of the state, and the apostolical hierarchy of the church of England, opposed to a whig.

Whig. The name of a faction. [Johnson, of course, belonged to the Tory party and despised the Whigs.]

Despite the humorous pedantry of the above definitions, Johnson adopted an enlightened and humble view about the relationship between language and lexicographers. "I am not yet so lost in lexicography, as to forget that words are the daughters of earth and that things are the sons of heaven," he wrote, and "Dictionaries are like watches: the worst is better than none, and the best cannot be expected to go quite true." For a while Johnson thought he was fixing the vocabulary in a final way, as the great academies of Italy and France imagined they had done. But the doctor's good sense came to his rescue, and in the superb preface to his dictionary he bowed to the truth about language and the human condition, a truth that he called "the immutable law of mutability":

> Those who have been persuaded to think well of my design, will require that it should fix our language, and put a stop to those alterations which time and chance have hitherto been suffered to make in it without opposition. With this consequence I will confess I have flattered myself for a while; but now begin to fear that I have indulged expectation which neither reason nor experience can justify. When we see men grow old and die at a certain time one after another, from century to century, we laugh at the elixir that promises to prolong life to a thousand years; and with equal justice may the lexicographer be derided, who, being able to produce no example of a nation that has preserved their words and phrases from mutability, shall imagine his dictionary can embalm his language, and secure it from corruption and decay. . . . Sounds are too volatile and subtle for legal restraints; to enchain syllables, and to lash the wind, are equally the undertakings of pride, unwilling to measure its desires by its strength.

Samuel Johnson's descriptive rather than prescriptive approach to language as something alive and changing made a lasting impression on succeeding generations of lexicographers. More than a century after Johnson's pathbreaking work, Sir James Murray, the great editor of the *Oxford English Dictionary*, echoed Johnson's practicality when he wrote, "It is a free country, and a man may call a vase a *vawse*, a *vahse*, a *vaze*, or a *vase*, as he pleases. And, why should he not? We do not all think alike, dress alike, write alike, or dine alike; why should we not use our liberty in speech also, so long as the purpose of speech, to be intelligible, and its grace, are not interfered with?''

Thanks to advances in the art of lexicography since the days of Dr. Johnson and to the flowering of the English language itself, unabridged dictionaries have burgeoned from the 43,000 entries in the *Dictionary of the English Language* to the more than 615,000 words in the current *Oxford English Dictionary*. Yet an entirely different kind of lexicon, and one that is but a fraction of the length of our big, fat unabridged dictionaries, has won the hearts of wordlovers throughout the English-speaking world. Although Ambrose Bierce's *The Devil's Dictionary*, published in 1911, contains scarcely more than a thousand entries set down on a mere one hundred thirty-eight pages, many of its readers insist that it is the most informative and penetrating dictionary ever produced.

Samuel Johnson and Ambrose Bierce could scarcely have been more different from one another. Johnson was born in Lichfield, England, in 1709. Bierce was born a farm boy in Meigs County, Ohio, in 1842. Johnson was disfigured, while Bierce was blessed with curly blond hair, bold mustache, blue piercing eyes, and striking good looks. His six-foot military bearing was so vital that young women breathlessly whispered that they could sense his presence across a room.

The convivial Johnson was often seen discoursing in the company of other great men and bending the elbow at the local pub. Bierce lived most of his life alone, and his powerful talents were always directed by bitterness and despair. His unremitting restlessness, his volatile temper, and his mysterious, suicidal death caused Clifton Fadiman to label Bierce a Voltaire with stomach ulcers.

Author of "An Occurrence at Owl Creek Bridge" and other macabre and unsettling short stories, Ambrose Bierce was widely hailed as "America's greatest cynic." He was this country's first successful syndicated newspaper columnist, and his column "Prattle" in the *San Francisco Examiner* contained some of the most withering wit, scorching sarcasm, and vituperative personal attacks that have ever been printed by an American newspaper. No wonder that he became known as Bitter Bierce.

Some critics tried to explain his lethal invective as the result of an unhappy, short-lived marriage to Mollie Day, a San Francisco society beauty. (See the definitions of *female* and *marriage*, below.) Others said Bierce's cynicism came from chronic rheumatism. His brother Albert felt that the cause was a terrible head wound that Ambrose received in the Civil War. Some asserted that Bierce's mean-spiritedness sprang from the absurdity of being born into a family in which each of twelve children was afflicted with a first name beginning with "A": Abigail, Addison, Albert, Almeda, Ambrose, and on and on. But Bierce's own feelings in the matter can be deduced from his definition of a cynic: "a blackguard whose faulty vision enables him to see things as they are!"

Despite their physical and emotional differences, Bierce is a direct, lineal descendant of Johnson, the fashioner of pithy, penetrating, and quirky definitions. Dr. Johnson defined *dull* as "not exhilarating; not delightful; as 'to make dictionaries is dull work.' " But

Johnson showed us that making dictionaries didn't have to be dull, and the irreverent, peripatetic life of Ambrose Bierce proved that lexicographers can be something very different from harmless drudges.

Between 1881 and 1906, Bierce, in his newspaper column, penned one deft, diabolical definition after another. These were eventually collected in 1911 in *The Devil's Dictionary*, addressed to those "enlightened souls who prefer dry wines to sweet, sense to sentiment, and wit to humour." Here are twenty of my favorite devilish definitions from Bitter Bierce's iconoclastic little lexicon:

Bacchus. A convenient deity invented by the ancients as an excuse for getting drunk.

bigot. One who is obstinately and zealously attached to an opinion that you do not entertain.

capital. The seat of misgovernment.

conservative. A statesman who is enamored of existing evils, as distinguished from the liberal, who wishes to replace them with others.

debauchee. One who has so earnestly pursued pleasure that he has had the misfortune to overtake it.

dentist. A prestidigitator who, putting metal in your mouth, pulls coins out of your pocket.

egotist. A person of low taste, more interested in himself than in me.

female. One of the opposing, or unfair sex.

friendship. A ship big enough to carry two in fair weather, but only one in foul.

happiness. An agreeable sensation arising from contemplating the misery of another.

history. An account mostly false, of events mostly unimportant, which are brought about by rulers mostly knaves and soldiers mostly fools.

learning. The kind of ignorance distinguishing the studious. [Bierce never went to school. What education he got he obtained from his father's books.]

marriage. The state or condition of a community consisting of a master, a mistress, and two slaves, making in all two.

mausoleum. The final and funniest folly of the rich.

Monday. In Christian countries, the day after the baseball game.

peace. In international affairs, a period of cheating between two periods of fighting.

politics. A strife of interests masquerading as a contest of principles. The conduct of public affairs for private advantage.

pray. To ask that the laws of the universe be annulled in behalf of a single petitioner confessedly unworthy.

saint. A dead sinner revised and edited.

year. A period of three hundred and sixty-five disappointments.

In 1912, at the age of seventy, Ambrose Bierce left for Mexico "with a pretty definite purpose, which, however, is not at present disclosable." Some say that he went off for one last glorious cause to fight beside Pancho Villa. Others say that, as a last desperate gesture, he turned his back on America and left for certain death in the midst of violent revolution. Whatever the facts, he simply vanished from life without a trace. The last words we have from him are contained in a letter he sent from Chihuahua, Mexico: "If you hear of my being stood up against a Mexican wall and shot to rags, please know that it is a pretty good way to depart this life. It beats old age, disease, or falling down the cellar stairs." Bierce may have departed the earthly stage without a trace, but the spirit of his caustic wordbook endures. Here are twenty additional cynical definitions conjured by some of Bitter Bierce's successors:

appeaser. One who feeds a crocodile hoping it will eat him last.—*Winston Churchill*

bargain. Something you can't use at a price you can't resist.—*Larry Laurence*

bore. A man who, when you ask him how he is, tells you.—*Bert Taylor*

camel. A horse that was planned by a committee. —Vogue *magazine*

celebrity. A person who works hard all his life to become well known and then wears dark glasses to avoid being recognized.—*Fred Allen*

committee. A group of men who keep minutes and waste hours.—*Milton Berle*

cricket. A game the British, not being a spiritual people, had to invent in order to have some conception of eternity.—*Lord Bancroft*

experience. A comb life gives you when you lose your hair.—*Judith Stern*

foreign aid. Taxing poor people in rich countries for the benefit of rich people in poor countries.—*Bernard Rosenberg*

heredity. The traits that a disobedient child gets from the other parent.—*Laurence Peter*

highbrow. The kind of person who looks at a sausage and thinks of Picasso. **lowbrow.** The kind of person who looks at Picasso and thinks of baloney. —*Leonard Levinson*

husband. What is left of a man after the nerve is extracted.—*Helen Rowland*

inflation. A process which allows you to live in a more expensive neighborhood without bothering to move.—*Craig Zellerbach*

memory. What tells a man his wife's birthday was yesterday.—*Mario Rocco*

politician. Any citizen with influence enough to get his old mother a job as charwoman at City Hall. —*H. L. Mencken*

specialist. A man who knows more and more about less and less.—*William Mayo*

synonym. A word used when you can't spell the word you want.—Chicago Daily Tribune

tact. The ability to tell a man he's open minded when he has a hole in his head.—*F. G. Kernan*

television. Chewing gum for the eyes.—*Frank Lloyd Wright*

vacation. When you spend thousands of dollars to see what rain looks like in a different part of the world.—*Robert Aiken*

Britain and America are dictionary nations. According to recent polls, ninety percent of all households in the two countries possess at least one dictionary, a higher percentage than those that own Bibles or cookbooks. That so many English speakers are not only literate but "dictionarate" is part of the inheritance handed down by a half-blind but far-sighted scholar laboring for nine years in a garret and his acerbic successor who used his piercing definitions to help define and elevate the art of satire.

THE WORD MAGIC
OF LEWIS
CARROLL

All in a golden afternoon
   Full leisurely we glide;
For both our oars, with little skill,
   By little arms are plied,
While little hands make vain pretence
Our wanderings to guide.

       . . .

Thus grew the tale of Wonderland:
   Thus slowly, one by one,
Its quaint events were hammered out—
   And now the tale is done,
And home we steer, a merry crew,
   Beneath the setting sun. . . .

On the fourth of July, 1862, a young Oxford don dressed in white flannels and straw boater took the day off to go a-rowing and go on a picnic with a Rev. Robinson Duckworth and three small girls. The don was Charles Lutwidge Dodgson, who was then, and for more than twenty-five years would remain, mathematical lecturer of Christ Church, and the girls were the daughters of Henry George Liddell, dean of the college. On that "golden afternoon" ten-year-old Alice Liddell, the middle of the three sisters, begged, "Tell us a story, please," and Dodgson began to spin a dreamtale about another little girl named Alice who followed a white rabbit down a hole and into another world. "Oh, Mr. Dodgson, I wish you would write out Alice's adventures for me," Alice Liddell said before the boating party disbanded. Dodgson granted her wish and in 1865 published *Alice's Adventures in Wonderland* under the pseudonym Lewis Carroll. Public response was so enthusiastic that the author was inspired to follow one masterpiece with another: *Through the Looking Glass* appeared in 1871.

The stories of Alice's tumble down a rabbit hole and her adventures on the other side of the mirror are the classics most widely read and adored by both children and adults alike. Carroll has become one of our most quoted authors, and the archetypal characters in his work have become imprinted on world folklore. Alexander Woollcott has written, "Not Tiny Tim, nor Falstaff, nor Rip Van Winkle, nor any other character wrought in the English tongue seems now a more permanent part of that tongue's heritage than do the high-handed Humpty Dumpty, the wistful Mad Hatter, the somewhat arbitrary Queen of Hearts, the evasive Cheshire Cat, and the gently pathetic White Knight." Why, we may ask, does the work of this girl-doting bachelor exert such a powerful hold on our collective imagination?

Although analyzing Carroll's fantasies is like trying to dissect a soap bubble, surely one source of their enduring appeal to children of all ages is their special sense of wonder about language. Just as Lewis Carroll, an adept amateur magician, made his life a brilliant entertainment through his parlor magic, so, in his writing, he created a magic show of words: words pulled out of hats, words sawed in half, words dancing in the air, words that disappear or show up in strange places and forms. Even his pen name is a complex anagram, Latinization, reversal, and retranslation of his Christian names: Charles Lutwidge to Edgar Cuthwellis to Carolus Ludovicus to Ludovicus Carolus to Lewis Carroll.

In his day-to-day life, Charles Lutwidge Dodgson was a classic Victorian fussbudget who, whatever the season, always wore gloves (just like the White Rabbit) and a top hat outdoors. He was possessed by a rage for order that bordered on the pathological. For fifty years he kept meticulous summaries of every letter he ever wrote or received, more than a hundred thousand of them, and maintained a record of the many luncheons and dinners he gave throughout his sociable lifetime, with diagrams showing where each guest sat and lists of just what dishes he had served. But in the brief fantasies he created as Lewis Carroll, this careful, ordered man challenged the fundamental assumptions of language and played hob with the basic order and structure of words.

Thus, in the Alice stories the young heroine declares that things are becoming "curiouser and curiouser," the Gryphon is disappointed that Alice, who knows what beautification is, does not know the meaning of *uglification*, and Humpty Dumpty receives an unbirthday present. In these examples, Carroll purposefully concocts eye-catching and ear-catching words by violating some of the basic conventions of word formation. *Curiouser* strikes us as curious because English speakers do not generally add the ending *-er* to three-syllable adjectives, *uglification* flies in the face of the rule that *-fication* can't be attached to adjectives like *ugly*, and *unbirthday* seems odd because we seldom prefix *-un* to nouns. (*Untruth* and *unrest* are two exceptions, but they involve nouns of one syllable.) Yet *curiouser* has come to inhabit the lunatic fringe of our language, and the memorableness of *unbirthday* has been exploited by a soft drink company that wants us to imbibe its "uncola."

Carroll showed a particular aptitude for making up blends by merging two words and beheading parts of one or both. He called these inventions portmanteau words because he loved to scrunch two words into one as clothes are crammed into a portmanteau, or traveling bag.

The most famous example of Lewis Carroll's facile gift for blending is his "Jabberwocky" poem, which begins:

'Twas brillig, and the slithy toves
    Did gyre and gimble in the wabe;
All mimsy were the borogoves,
    And the mome raths outgrabe.

When Alice asks Humpty Dumpty to explain the word *slithy*, he answers: "Well, *slithy* means 'lithe and slimy. . . .' You see, it's like a portmanteau—there are two meanings packed up into one word." Dumpty later interprets *mimsy*: "Well then, *mimsy* is 'flimsy and miserable' (there's another portmanteau for you)." Two words that appear later in "Jabberwocky" have become enshrined in dictionaries of the English language—*chortle* ("chuckle" + "snort") and *galumph* ("gallop" + "triumph"). When we today eat Frogurt, drink Cranapple juice, and chew Dynamints, we are sharing Lewis Carroll's delight with portmanteau words.

He often played with the eccentric logic of discourse, as we see in "A Mad Tea-Party":

> "Then you should say what you mean," the March Hare went on.
>
> "I do," Alice hastily replied; "at least—at least I mean what I say—that's the same thing, you know."
>
> "Not the same thing a bit!" said the Hatter. "Why, you might just as well say that 'I see what I eat' is the same thing as 'I eat what I see'! . . ."
>
> "Take some more tea," the March Hare said to Alice, very earnestly.
>
> "I've had nothing yet," Alice replied in an offended tone, "so I can't take more."
>
> "You mean you can't take *less*," said the Hatter; "it's very easy to take *more* than nothing."

During the years in which Lewis Carroll was standing language and logic on their heads, C. L. Dodgson was publishing mathematical works, the most famous of these being *Euclid and His Modern Rivals* (1879). Besides the *Alice* and *Snark* books, the forms of Lewis Carroll's creativity ranged from whimsical entertainment to mathematical riddles. Puzzles, games, logistic contortions, and symbolic manipulations leapt from his mind and into print, much to the pleasure of the English drawing-room set. He wrote, "Mental recreation is a thing that we all need for our mental health," and he left his readers' heads spinning with such word games as Mischmasch, Lanrick, and Syzygies, all based on the rule that by changing a letter in a word, a different word can be produced. His most popular word game, Doublets, was published regularly in *Vanity Fair* and became the rage of the 1870s. Here are some of Carroll's doublets, with directions as printed in *Vanity Fair*:

1. The words given to be linked together constitute a "Doublet." The interposed words are "links." The entire series is a "chain." The object is to complete the chain with the required number of links.

2. Each word in the chain must be formed from the preceding word by changing one letter in it, and only one. The substituted letter occupied in the preceding word, and all the other letters must retain their places.

One example that Carroll offered was the transmutation of HEAD to TAIL: HEAD-heal-teal-tell-tall-TAIL. In various *Vanity Fair* articles Carroll posed these additional challenges: 1. Drive PIG into STY. 2. Raise FOUR to FIVE. 3. Evolve MAN from APE. Answers repose at the end of this chapter.

Perhaps the most profound significance of Carroll's topsy-turvy world is contained in his attitude toward the very function of language, as seen in Chapter 6 of *Through the Looking Glass*. Alice complains to Humpty Dumpty, the large, articulate egg (soon to be an omelette): "I don't know what you mean by 'glory' ":

Humpty Dumpty smiled contemptuously. "Of course you don't—till I tell you. I meant 'there's a nice knock-down argument for you!' "

"But 'glory' doesn't mean 'a nice knock-down argument,' " Alice objected.

"When *I* use a word," Humpty Dumpty said, in a rather scornful tone, "it means just what I choose it to mean—neither more nor less."

"The question is," said Alice, "whether you *can* make words mean so many different things."

"The question is," said Humpty Dumpty, "which is the master—that's all."

Such banter may sound like sheer nonsense, yet in its way it is quite profound. On the one side, Alice insists that there are limits to our freedom with words, that if you use *glory* to mean "a nice knock-down argument," rather than "fame" or "honor," no one will know what you are talking about. After all, if you mean "no" when you say "yes," you will appear to be a fool or a liar. If you use *hat* to mean "shoes," you are likely to get cold feet. But on the other side, Humpty Dumpty is also right, for Alice's attitude that words can signify only what the dictionary says they do means thinking of language as being very rigid indeed. Carried to an extreme, Alice's philosophy rules out the use of irony, slang, fanciful words, and new expressive terms. After all, when somebody spills hot soup on your new suit or dress and you say, "That was a smart move," you are not using *smart* in any dictionary sense. When someone at some point decided that *Mickey Mouse* could mean "trivial or unworthy," rather than just the name of an animated cartoon star, he or she invented a meaning that was not enshrined in our lexicons.

Real, everyday language, then, is the result of a give-and-take between originality and the dictionary, an eternal dialectic between Humpty Dumpty and Alice. As Lewis Carroll and his thin-shelled spokesegg realized, words are living, changing reflections of human attitudes, not dead and petrified artifacts. As long as we human beings remain alive, we shall shape, stretch, and re-create our language. And we shall draw delight and wisdom from the fantasies written by the shy Oxford don whose adopted name has become a synonym for a very special kind of magic.

Answers to Doublets: 1. PIG-wig-wag-way-say-STY 2. FOUR-foul-fool-foot-fort-fore-fire-FIVE 3. APE-are-ere-err-ear-mar-MAN.

THE YEAR OF MARK TWAIN

In 1920 Babe Ruth compiled a slugging average of .847, and ten years later Hack Wilson batted in one hundred ninety runs. In 1961 Roger Maris belted sixty-one home runs and Wilt Chamberlain began an NBA season in which his scoring average was 50.4 points. In 1972 the Miami Dolphins went through an NFL season undefeated at 17–0, and in 1984 Dolphins quarterback Dan Marino threw forty-eight touchdown passes.

These are stellar, perhaps even unsurpassable, records—but has there ever been a year like the one Mark Twain had in 1985? In that year of chronological confluences, we marked the centennial anniversary of the American publication of *The Adventures of Huckleberry Finn*, the sesquicentennial of the birth of its author, Mark Twain, and the seventy-fifth anniversary of his death. And—yet a fourth coincidence—an old celestial friend of Twain's returned to help celebrate this rare conjunction of the stars.

In *Mark Twain's Autobiography* Samuel Langhorne Clemens tells us that he "was born the 30th of

November, 1835, in the almost invisible village of Florida, Missouri." As a barefoot boy sitting on the banks of the Mississippi River, he watched stern-wheeler boats churning the muddy waters, and he heard the leadsmen sounding the depth of the river by calling out to the captains, "By the deep six . . . by the mark five . . . by the deep four . . . by the mark three." When the river bottom was only two fathoms, or twelve feet, down, he would hear the lusty cry "by the mark twain." Long after he left the Mississippi, and after various careers as a riverboat pilot, prospector, and printer, Sam Clemens, now a journalist, contributed an article to the *Nevada Territorial Enterprise* on February 3, 1865, and signed it with a new name—Mark Twain.

In 1876 Twain published *The Adventures of Tom Sawyer*, a novel that reached back into his Missouri childhood. Later that year, in a casual note written to William Dean Howells, Twain mentioned that he had begun "another boy's book—more to be at work than anything else. I have written 400 pages on it—therefore it is very nearly half done. It is Huckleberry Finn's Autobiography. I like it only tolerably well, as far as I have got, and may possibly pigeonhole or burn the MS when it is done."

Fortunately Twain did not destroy his text, and on February 18, 1885, thirty thousand copies of *The Adventures of Huckleberry Finn* were released in the United States. The book was supposed to have come out in December 1884, but, as if the fates knew that such a release date would have imperiled the great anniversary year Twain was to have in 1985, production problems delayed publication for two months.

The novel turned out to be Twain's masterpiece,

and it changed the direction of American letters. Ernest Hemingway spoke for generations of twentieth-century American writers when he said, "All modern American literature comes from one book by Mark Twain called *Huckleberry Finn*. There was nothing before. There has been nothing as good since." With *Huckleberry Finn* American literature came of age.

"You don't know about me, without you have read a book by the name of *The Adventures of Tom Sawyer*, but that ain't no matter. That book was made by Mr. Mark Twain and he told the truth, mainly. There was things which he stretched, but mainly he told the truth." With these sentences Mark Twain not only began his finest novel but uttered a clarion call for a new way of writing. In *The Adventures of Huckleberry Finn*, Twain used seven distinct dialects to reflect the speech patterns of various characters, and he also became the first important author to capture the freshness and vitality of the newly hewn American idiom in narrative as well as dialogue. Just as Geoffrey Chaucer's *The Canterbury Tales* is the first significant work written in English, *Huckleberry Finn* is the first novel of world rank to be written entirely in American.

To see what Twain accomplished, compare the diction of his book with that of Nathaniel Hawthorne's *The Scarlet Letter*, published only thirty-five years earlier. Listen first to little Pearl, the small daughter of Hester Prynne: "Nay, mother, I have told all I know. Ask yonder old man whom thou hast been talking with! It may be he can tell. But in good earnest now, mother dear, what does this scarlet letter mean?—and why dost thou wear it on thy bosom?" Does that sound like the language of a young American girl? Has any child anywhere ever talked like that?

Now hear Huck Finn:

> The first thing to see, looking away over the water, was a kind of dull line—that was the woods, on t'other side—you couldn't make nothing else out; then a pale place in the sky; then more paleness spreading around; then the river softened up away off, and warn't black any more, but gray; you could see little dark spots drifting along, ever so far away—trading scows and such things; and long black streaks—rafts; sometimes you could hear a sweep screaking; or jumbled up voices, it was so still, and sounds come so far; and by-and-by you could see a streak on the water which you know by the look of the streak that there's a snag in a swift current which breaks on it and makes that streak look that way; then the nice breeze springs up, and comes fanning you from over there, so cool and fresh, and sweet to smell, on account of the woods and flowers; but sometimes not that way, because they've left dead fish laying around, gars, and such, and they do get pretty rank; and next you've got the full day, and everything smiling in the sun, and the song-birds just going it!

That is pure, unalloyed American folk poetry, freed from the straitjacket of literary prose. That is the writing of a man who, in 1885, wrote in his notebook, "My works are like water. The works of the great masters are like wine. But everyone drinks water." That is style stripped of all illusion and puffery. Has anyone else ever tapped as deeply the easy grace and direct simplicity of American speech?

Twain held strong opinions about a passel of subjects, and he possessed the gift of being able to state these views in memorable ways: "It's better to keep your mouth shut and appear stupid than to open it and remove all doubt"; "Be careful about reading health books. You may die of a misprint"; "It's easy to give up smoking; I've done it many times." He also had a lot to say about style, literature, and the American language that he, more than any other writer, helped to shape:

On American English, compared with British English

The property has gone into the hands of a joint stock company, and we own the bulk of the shares.

On dialects

I have traveled more than anyone else, and I have noticed that even the angels speak English with an accent.

On choosing words

The difference between the almost right word and the right word is really a large matter—'tis the difference between the lightning-bug and the lightning.

More on word choice

A powerful agent is the right word: it lights the reader's way and makes it plain. A close approximation to it will answer, and much traveling is done in a well-enough fashion by its help, but we do not welcome it and rejoice in it as we do when the right word blazes out at us. Whenever we come upon one of these intensely right words in a book or a newspaper, the resulting effect is physical as well as spiritual, and electrically prompt. It tingles exquisitely around through the walls of the mouth and tastes as tart and crisp and good as the autumn butter that creams the sumac berry.

On style (in a letter to a twelve-year-old boy)

I notice that you use plain, simple language, short words, and brief sentences. That is the way to write English—it is the modern way and the best way. Stick to it; and don't let fluff and flowers and verbosity creep in.

When you catch an adjective, kill it. No, I don't mean utterly, but kill most of them—then the rest will be valuable. They weaken when they are close together. They give strength when they are wide apart.

On being concise

With a hundred words to do it with, the literary

artisan could catch that airy thought and tie it down and reduce it to a . . . cabbage, but the artist does it with twenty, and the result is a flower.

More on conciseness

A successful book is not made of what is in it, but what is left out of it.

On using short words

I never write *metropolis* for seven cents when I can get the same for *city*. I never write *policeman* because I can get the same for *cop*.

More on short words

Eschew surplusage.

On the first-person-plural pronoun

Only presidents, editors, and people with tapeworms ought to have the right to use the editorial *we*.

On clichés

Adam was the only man who, when he said a good thing, knew that nobody had said it before him.

On grammar

Perfect grammar—persistent, continuous, sustained—is the fourth dimension, so to speak. Many have sought it, but none has found it. . . . I know grammar by ear only, not by note, not by rules. A generation ago I knew the rules—knew them by heart, word for word, though not their meanings—and I still know one of them: the one which says—which says—but never mind, it will come back to me presently.

On spelling

I don't see any use in having a uniform and arbitrary way of spelling words. We might as well make all clothing alike and cook all dishes alike. Sameness is tiresome; variety is pleasure. *Kow* spelled with a large *K* is just as good as with a small *c*. It is better. It gives the imagination a broader field, a wider scope.

On spelling reform

Simplified spelling is all right, but, like chastity, you can carry it too far.

On literature

A classic is something that everybody wants to have read but nobody wants to read.

On reading

The man who does not read good books has no advantage over the man who can't read them.

On dictionaries

A Dictionary is the most awe-inspiring of all books; it knows so much. . . . It has gone around the sun, and spied out everything and lit it up.

On speaking

It usually takes more than three weeks to prepare a good impromptu speech.

On sermonizing

Few sinners are saved after the first twenty minutes of a sermon.

On writing humor

There are several kinds of stories, but only one difficult kind—the humorous.

On nonsense literature

It takes a heap of sense to write good nonsense.

Of all the witty statements that Mark Twain said or wrote, none has been quoted more often than his terse response to an alarmist report. Twain was on a visit to London, where he was to be the guest of honor at a literary club dinner. Early in the day the affair was to take place the secretary of the club was shocked to hear the news that Twain had died suddenly. The distraught officer sought to verify the facts by a diplomatic note to Mrs. Clemens in which he mentioned the whispers of her husband's demise. Twain got hold of the note and telegraphed the now-famous reply: "The reports of my death are greatly exaggerated." The inscription appears on his gravestone in Elmira, New York.

On April 21, 1910, Twain did, without exaggeration, pass on. At the funeral, his friend William Dean Howells came up to say good-bye: "I looked a moment at the face I knew so well; and it was patient with the patience I had so often seen in it; something of a puzzle, a great silent dignity, an assent to what must be from the depths of a nature whose tragical seriousness broke in the laughter which the unwise took for the whole of him." In *My Mark Twain*, published the year of his friend's death, Howells added: "Emerson, Longfellow, Lowell, Holmes—I knew them all—sages, poets, seers, critics, humorists; they were like one another and like other literary men; but Clemens was sole, incomparable, the Lincoln of our literature."

On the night before Twain's death, Halley's Comet shone in the skies as it made its closest approach to the earth. Just a year before, Twain had said to a friend: "I came in with Halley's Comet in 1835. It is coming again next year, and I expect to go out with it. It will be the greatest disappointment of my life if I don't go with Halley's Comet. The almighty has said, no doubt, 'Now here go those two unaccountable frauds; they came in together, they must go out together.' Oh! I am looking forward to that."

In December 1985 Halley's Comet once again began its journey across our heavens, a brilliant reminder of the birth, work, and death of Mark Twain—humorist, lecturer, storyteller, social commentator, artist—the writer who gave a young nation a voice to sing of itself.

THE HILLTOP OF THE HEART

When she died on May 15, 1886, no one alive, least of all she herself, dared imagine that she would become recognized as one of the most original of all American poets. When she died, in Amherst, Massachusetts, none of her contemporaries dreamed that she would one day be ranked among the greatest poets who ever used the English language. To them she cast a small, pale shadow when measured against the American giants of her time—Longfellow, Whittier, and Lowell. Yet those poets are hardly read at all today, while she, living alone and unattended, sings to us across the years and continues to influence the course of twentieth-century verse.

Emily Dickinson lived what appeared to be a reclusive, invisible, and inaudible life. Dressed in the symbolic white that she ever afterward wore, she gradually withdrew into her home and garden, and scarcely ever left. No one knows why.

She described herself as "small, like the wren, and my hair is bold, like the chestnut burr; and my eyes like the sherry glasses that the guests leave behind." But those eyes of hers, which she pictured as discarded, used-up objects, were brimful with a dazzling vision. As Robert Frost once remarked about her, "To write about falling water, one doesn't have to go to Niagara":

I never saw a Moor—
I never saw the Sea—
Yet know I how the heather looks
And what a billow be.

I never spoke with God—
Nor visited in heaven—
Yet certain am I of the spot
As if the Checks were given.

Emily Dickinson never wrote anything big, like a novel or a play or a long poem. But year after year, on odd scraps of paper and the backs of envelopes, she composed 1,775 little things, "tied together with twine in sixty little bundles." Within the tight confines of the hymnal stanza she knew so well from church and within the boundaries of the garden she came increasingly to inhabit, she used language to explore the trackless reaches of the human condition.

Like her garden, she cultivated her poetry for her own pleasure, not for public display. "Publication is the auction of the mind," she wrote in a letter. She never arranged her poems in any order, and she never gave them titles. Only seven were published during her lifetime, and they anonymously. She seemed afraid that fame, even posthumous fame, would brush her with its wings, and she left instructions for all her manuscripts to be destroyed:

> I'm Nobody! Who are you?
> Are you—Nobody—too?
> Then there's a pair of us!—don't tell!
> They'd banish us—you know!
>
> How dreary—to be—Somebody!
> How public—like a Frog—
> To tell your name—the livelong June—
> To an admiring Bog!

Such methodical arrangements for obscurity would seem to have been perfect. Yet they failed. Emily Dickinson may have hidden her life from public view, but she could not bury her genius. Today, a little more than a century after her death, we still find ourselves responding to her strange and beautiful verse.

She wrote that the poet "Distills amazing sense/ From ordinary Meanings." That is just what she does: she catches with language the sense of the miraculous in occurrences that appear to be common—the grass springing from the earth, a robin eating a worm, a bee floating above a flower, and even a snake coiling its path:

> A narrow Fellow in the Grass
> Occasionally rides—
> You may have met Him—did you not
> His notice sudden is—

The Grass divides as with a Comb—
A spotted shaft is seen—
And then it closes at your feet
And opens further on—

Louis Untermeyer once wrote that "poetry is the power of defining the indefinable in terms of the unforgettable." Nothing that the poet does is more important than creating moments of pure emotional clarity and insight into things and actions that are close at hand, even if we don't always notice them. Emily Dickinson makes her readers feel deeply about something as indefinable and impalpable as the dying light of a winter afternoon, a light that is scarcely a light at all:

There's a certain Slant of Light,
Winter Afternoons—
That oppresses, like the Heft
Of Cathedral Tunes—

When the poem was first published in 1890, the editors substituted "weight" for "heft" and thus quietly ruined it. They desecrated the pungent colloquialness of *heft* and changed the meaning. In her poem, *heft* conveys simultaneously the sense of heaviness, of weight pressing down, and of lifting up, of heaving. *Heft* means not only a heavy weight but also the straining effort to lift such a weight (to heave it upward: *heave* and *heavy* come from the same root). Just as the plangent music of a church organ both weighs down upon our spirit and lifts us toward the eternal, the slant of light late of a winter afternoon reminds us

of our brief tenure in this life and bestirs us to shake
off the icy grip of wintry death.

Each year in my modern poetry course I ask my
students to create poems in the style of Emily Dickinson. As living testaments to the powerful spell that the
Belle of Amherst still casts upon lovers of poetry, my
students again and again capture and crystallize Dickinson's hymnal rhythms, slant rhymes, feeling for
color and sound, and intuition of the miraculous in the
near-at-hand:

I Felt a Curious Tickle

I felt a curious tickle feel
Its way across my arm.
Its plate of armor caught the light
And gave away alarm.

The weary warrior kept its pace—
Not bold, but shy and poised;
Meandering from post to post,
It crept, then quickly froze.

A glance shot up quite timidly—
A quick stare from beneath
The tranquil, iridescent shell
Of black, indigo, green.

My laugh it fell, the wobble thrust
The scarab off its claws.
The brave centurion spread its wings;
A blur was all I saw.
                              —*Jennifer Horne*

Emily Dickinson wrote many poems about death. While most of her contemporaries described death in mawkish clichés as rude, sudden, and impersonal, she transformed him into a kindly and patient gentleman caller. Seeing that the speaker in "Because I Could Not Stop for Death" is caught up in the hum and buzz of her earthly life, Death comes by her house and pays a leisurely visit:

> Because I could not stop for Death—
> He kindly stopped for me—
> The Carriage held but just Ourselves—
> And Immortality.
>
> We slowly drove—He knew no haste,
> And I had put away
> My labor and my leisure too,
> For his Civility—

Death's carriage came to stop at Emily's house on May 15, 1886. Using the hymnal stanza that Dickinson so loved, the poet Melville Cane has written her a luminous epitaph:

> Inclosed within a hedge
> Of privet, doubts and nays,
> A burning spinster paced
> Her clipped New England days.
>
> While pretty singers droned
> A local, nasal hymn,

She raised a timeless voice;
It reached a spatial rim.

She never saw a moor.
She never saw the sea.
Yet from a hilltop in her heart
She scanned infinity.

THE LEGACY OF
T. S. ELIOT

Perhaps the greatest poet of the twentieth century, T. S. Eliot is also one of its greatest paradoxes. The man who considered himself a New England poet was born in St. Louis, on September 16, 1888, to a local merchant and a former New England schoolteacher. His paternal grandfather, a Unitarian minister, had gone west from Massachusetts, and Eliot returned to that state in 1904 to attend Milton Academy and Harvard College. In 1915 Eliot left the United States, studied at Oxford, settled in London, and, in 1927, acquired British citizenship and joined the Church of England. Habitually wearing a bowler hat and carrying a malacca stick and furled umbrella, the man who was born in the very center of the United States ultimately became more British than most Britishers.

He was descended from a distinguished line of historic personages: One ancestor, Thomas Elyot, had openly reproved Henry VIII on account of Anne Boleyn; another forebear, Andrew Eliot, had officiated at the Salem, Massachusetts, witch trials. Yet Thomas Stearns Eliot was one of the first poets to write about the effects of the megalopolis on modern life: "Unreal City/Under the brown fog of a winter noon." His demeanor was forbiddingly serious and formal—hooded, introspective eyes set in a pale, sculptured face—yet in the sunset of his life he married a woman thirty years younger than he and struck up a friendship with Groucho Marx. Although, for most readers, Eliot's poetry is often elusive and inaccessibly allusive, millions know him through the hit musical *Cats*, which is based on his humorous collection of poems, *Old Possum's Book of Practical Cats*. But T. S. Eliot was a literary natural resource who was much more than a gold mine of Broadway revenue.

When he died in London on January 5, 1965, the Massachusetts writer John Updike justly expressed the impact of that loss: "The death of T. S. Eliot deprives the English-speaking world not only of a literary master but of a cultural presence that united two literatures and extended the venerable tradition of the presiding poet-critic into the present time. He was our Dryden, our Coleridge, our Arnold; and as long as he was alive, our literature seemed in some way restrained from the apocalyptic formlessness that it seeks."

That Eliot continues to live among us as a "cultural presence" is evident in the extent to which his voice suffuses the way we speak and write. He may not be widely read these days, but his language and imagery stock our thoughts. In 1982 *Time* magazine ran a profile of Jean Harris, the private-school headmistress who had been imprisoned for the death of Scarsdale diet doctor Herman Tarnower. The article began: "Jean Struven Harris behind bars is a study in incongruities.

She once ran her own kingdom, the Madeira School, where heed was paid and homage given to the headmistress. She once presided over gourmet luncheons, toast and tea, with women who would come and go, talking of Michelangelo."

This last sentence is an elegant allusion to Eliot's "The Love Song of J. Alfred Prufrock" and flashes a revelatory light on Jean Harris's former life. First published in 1910, "The Love Song" illuminates the character of proper Bostonian J. Alfred Prufrock in order to probe the spiritual dilemmas of desiccated people amidst the alienation of life in the twentieth century. Early in his monologue Prufrock, utterly unable to make decisions, sighs:

> . . . There will be time, there will be time
> To prepare a face to meet the faces that you meet; . . .
> And time yet for a hundred indecisions,
> And for a hundred visions and revisions,
> Before the taking of a toast and tea.

And the hollow, jinglelike refrain that echoes Prufrock's life and his "love song" skips along:

> In the room the women come and go
> Talking of Michelangelo.

In a 1989 issue of *Time* the title of the cover story of the dangers of pesticides asked, "Do You Dare to Eat a Peach?" The spiritually bereft Prufrock doesn't dare: A peach, after all, is round and fleshy and downed with light hair; in the biting, Prufrock risks having the juice run down his chin and striking his teeth on the embedded pit:

Shall I part my hair behind? Do I dare to eat a peach?
I shall wear white flannel trousers, and walk upon the
    beach.

Ralph Jimenez, a science writer for our local newspaper, began a column on sea legs with this sentence:
"The crabmeat in most seafood salads never spent any
time in a pair of ragged claws scuttling across the floors
of silent seas. It was made in a blender." This is a witty
reference to another couplet in "The Love Song of J.
Alfred Prufrock." Rather than be the spiritually dead
man he actually is, Prufrock wishes that he were some
primitive sea creature—all claws, alive as only instinc-
tive, brute force:

I should have been a pair of ragged claws
Scuttling across the floors of silent seas.

Many a story and editorial about income tax time
begins "April is the cruelest month," quoting, know-
ingly or otherwise, the first line of Eliot's epic "The
Waste Land," which in 1922 established his worldwide
fame. The very title of "The Waste Land" has become
a code word for the spiritual loss and distress of indus-
trialized society since World War I.

In May of 1987 television critic Tom Shales wrote
an elegy on the final episode of "Hill Street Blues,"
stating that the distinguished show "does not go out
with a bang, but hardly with a whimper either." Less
than a month later Mike Downey described the effect
of an unusually physical and acrimonious seven-game
playoff between the Boston Celtics and Detroit Pistons:
"So, the series ended with bangs and whimpers."

Here both writers are playing with the ending of Eliot's "The Hollow Men" (1923):

> This is the way the world ends
> This is the way the world ends
> This is the way the world ends
> Not with a bang but a whimper.

"Not with a bang but a whimper" may be the most widely quoted line in the poetry of this century. For hollow men, "Leaning together/Headpiece filled with straw," the world will expire not with a paroxysm of violence but from the inertia of ennui and apathy.

In recognition of his titanic contribution to modern poetry, T. S. Eliot was awarded the Nobel Prize for literature in 1948. No one has expressed more articulately the spirit of an age littered by the shards of broken philosophies; no one has striven harder to make the vessel of the human condition whole once more. "When a poet's mind is perfectly equipped for its work," he wrote, "it is constantly amalgamating disparate experience. The ordinary man's experience is chaotic, irregular, fragmentary. The latter falls in love, or reads Spinoza, and these two experiences have nothing to do with each other, or with the noise of the typewriter or the smell of cooking; in the mind of the poet these experiences are always forming new wholes." Eliot taught us that all experiences and all emotions coalesce into a seamless whole. He showed that the poet can cast large ideas in the language of everyday parlance. His work is testimony that an artist can be, at the same time, intellectually brilliant and deeply emotional, even passionate.

GEORGE ORWELL IS WATCHING YOU

I wish that *Nineteen Eighty-Four* weren't called *Nineteen Eighty-Four*.*

I can understand why George Orwell chose that title for his final and most famous novel. Reversing the last two digits of 1948, the year in which he wrote much of the book, he wanted to show that within a single generation democracy and freedom could vanish from history to be replaced by an all-controlling tyranny. He wanted to warn a world just beginning to feel the long winter of the Cold War that a Big Brother state could enter the innermost recesses of the human spirit and destroy it.

Still, I wish Orwell had come up with a title like *Twenty Twenty-Four* or *Twenty Eighty-Four*. Then, people would still be reading the book by the millions, as they did during the first thirty-five years of its life, when it caught the attention of readers throughout the

---

*Orwell spelled out his title, and the practice was followed in the first editions of the book.

146

world—at least in those parts of the world where people were free to read the books they chose. Now that the actual year 1984 has come and gone, and now that the Iron Curtain has lifted to expose so many shriveled totalitarian states, relatively few readers experience the chilling prophecies of Orwell's dystopian vision.

"From a very early age, perhaps the age of five or six, I knew that when I grew up I should be a writer," Orwell recorded, and his life was one long preparation for the writing of *Nineteen Eighty-Four*. He was born in 1903 as Eric Arthur Blair at Motihari, in Bengal, India, where his father was a civil servant of the British empire. Brilliant but poor, the tall, gaunt boy won a scholarship to Eton and grew up, as he said, "an odious young snob." In the early 1930s he changed his name to George Orwell because he liked the Englishness of *George* and had grown fond of the River Orwell, near which he was living at the time.

After a five-year hitch as a sergeant with the Imperial Indian Police in Burma, the ultimate symbol of British colonialism, he returned to the European continent in 1927. He broke away from his family and his past and deliberately cast his lot with laborers and beggars, living as an impoverished socialist in London and Paris. In 1936 he went to Spain to report on the Spanish Civil War. There he joined the Loyalist forces against the Fascist troops, suffered a bullet wound in the neck, and observed the cynical playing with human life in which "leaders" on both sides indulged.

After returning to England in 1937, he worked for the BBC until 1944, when he became literary editor of the Socialist *London Tribune*. During his tenure with the *Tribune*, Orwell wrote "Politics and the English

Language," which has become the most reprinted of all English essays. In it he discusses the parlous condition of the English language and exposes the prevalent diseases that afflict it: "Modern English prose . . . consists less and less of *words* chosen for the sake of their meaning, and more and more of *phrases* tacked together like the sections of a prefabricated henhouse." Orwell catalogs and analyzes various types of rhetorical "swindles and perversions," concluding that "the great enemy of clear language is insincerity. When there is a gap between one's real and one's declared aims, one turns as it were instinctively to long words and exhausted idioms, like a cuttlefish squirting out ink." As an example of the kind of ink verbal insincerity can so easily squirt, Orwell quotes a well-known verse from Ecclesiastes:

> I returned and saw under the sun, that the race is not to the swift, nor the battle to the strong, neither yet bread to the wise, nor yet riches to men of understanding, nor yet favour to men of skill; but time and chance happeneth to all of them.

Then the essayist presents a version of the passage with its lifeblood drained away and replaced by the embalming fluid of modern English style:

> Objective consideration of contemporary phenomena compels the conclusion that success or failure in competitive activities exhibits no tendency to be commensurate with innate capacity, but that a considerable element of the unpredictable must invariably be taken into account.

The biblical passage contains sixty syllables, the "translation" ninety. Yet which version, asks Orwell, seems fresher and more vivid? More telling, which seems closer to the kind of speech and writing we encounter in modern times?

Orwell doesn't just complain. He states that "the decadence of our language is probably curable" and ends his essay by suggesting a number of remedies to help restore the language to a healthier state. For a set of rules for plain talk and clear writing, it would be difficult to better these six offered in "Politics and the English Language." If we all followed these guidelines, our prose might not be as good as Orwell's, but it would certainly be to the point:

1. Never use a metaphor, simile, or other figure of speech which you are used to seeing in print.

2. Never use a long word where a short one will do.

3. If it is possible to cut a word out, always cut it out.

4. Never use the passive where you can use the active.

5. Never use a foreign phrase, a scientific word, or a jargon word if you can think of an everyday English equivalent.

6. Break any of these rules sooner than say anything outright barbarous.

George Orwell was fanatical about clarity in writing: "So long as I remain alive and well, I shall continue to feel strongly about prose style," he wrote. His ideal style, for the political purposes that claimed all his attention, is explained in the simile "Good prose is like a window-pane." In that phrase we see not merely the quality of his writing but, as a man who always valued ideals above ideologies, the personal integrity that went into its making. Writes Laurence Brander, Orwell's colleague at the BBC, "He had one gift, which will be the envy of all who study him: the gift of writing prose. He had the character to preserve that gift and to use it for the benefit of society."

It was in his last book that Orwell most forcefully carried on two of the great traditions in English writing—unshakable individualism and a passion for prose style. In 1949, as he lay on a sanatorium bed under the shadow of a death that would soon come from tuberculosis and exhaustion, the world received *Nineteen Eighty-Four* and gained a new synonym for tyranny and totalitarianism.

In Orwell's nightmare vision the world, after an atomic war, has divided itself into three massive slave states—Oceania, Eurasia, and Eastasia. The three superpowers are about equal in strength and are continuously at war. But it is a war that nobody can win.

In the hands of the governments absolute power has corrupted absolutely. Power is exercised not for the salvation of the State or the benefit of its subjects, but for its own sake, as an end in itself. Each dictatorship possesses an all-pervading control of collective behavior and of thought itself. The past is a pawn in the hands of present policy: When the rulers want to change history, they destroy all old books and periodicals and replace them with new ones. The power elite is cynically indifferent to truth. In effect, there is no truth and there is no past.

It is the same with people. Dissent is outlawed. Citizens who dare to think antistate thoughts are branded "unpersons" and sent off to "unexist" or be brutally re-educated.

The line is rigidly set by Big Brother, the black-mustachioed dictator whose dark, penetrating eyes stare down from posters everywhere. The flunkies of Big Brother's party are supervised by two-way tele-screens in all rooms and public places. BIG BROTHER IS WATCHING YOU. A wrong facial expression can mean liquidation; there is no such thing as a private life.

But what of the words and phrases that persist in the citizens' minds? These have been labeled Crime-think, and the greatest of all thought crimes is called Ownlife. Crimethink is being stamped out by Double-think, which teaches by numbing repetition the three slogans of the party:

WAR IS PEACE

FREEDOM IS SLAVERY

IGNORANCE IS STRENGTH

Doublethink is a mere preparation for Newspeak, a modified form of Oldspeak, or standard English, designed with catchall clichés and fewer words so as to make reflective, creative, and unorthodox thought impossible. Just as Shakespeare and the rest of the classics have been eviscerated through translation into Newspeak, so the minds of the citizens are constantly being re-edited through successive editions of the Newspeak dictionary.

Nineteen Eighty-Four is the story of Winston

Smith, "a smallish, frail figure," who lives in London, the major city of Airstrip One, as Britain is then called, in the superstate of Oceania. In the course of the story Smith, a clerk in the Ministry of Truth, commits the enormous crime of falling in love with a woman who, like him, opposes the system. Inevitably discovered and arrested by the Thought Police, the two lovers undergo long periods of re-education through the Ministry of Love.* Released years later as a rehabilitated member of society, Smith learns to love Big Brother and not only to admit that 2 plus 2 is 5, but to believe it with all that is left of his heart and soul. "Whatever the Party holds to be truth *is* truth. It is impossible to see reality except by looking through the eyes of the Party."

For many readers, the most terrifying aspect of *Nineteen Eighty-Four* is not the technological gimmick of the two-way telescreens, but the government's ability to engird thought by restricting its vehicle, language. Orwell emphasizes again and again the iron link between language and mind. If our words are the windows through which we look at the world, reducing the number and size of those windows limits our ability to view and deal with reality.

Of Orwell's death Laurence Brander has written, "Fate was malicious, as much to us as to him, when it chose that moment in January, 1950, to end 'the thin-spun life.' " Beyond that shortened life we can sense

---

*The Ministry of Truth and Ministry of Love are Doublethink labels for the Ministry of Propaganda and the Ministry of Brainwashing. As transparent as these titles appear to be, we must note that, in 1949, the year *Nineteen Eighty-Four* was published, the United States Department of War suddenly became the Department of Defense.

Orwell's presence in the way he pervades our thoughts and our vocabulary. The adjective *Orwellian*, the four neutral numbers *1984*, and the catchphrase "Big Brother Is Watching You" have been branded so long on public consciousness that they have acquired the power of hieroglyphs for totalitarianism and repression.

In inventing the word *Newspeak*, Orwell gave the English language a new meaning-bearing element, a combining root that now describes the specialized vocabularies of various activities, interests, and occupations. Among the coinages collected over the past two decades are *adspeak*, *artspeak*, *discospeak*, *edspeak*, *splitspeak*, *sportspeak*, *teenspeak*, *valleyspeak*, *warspeak*, and, perhaps the best-known derivative, *nukespeak*. In a 1990 *Boston Globe* magazine article, John Powers fabricated the term *bitespeak* to label the debased English we use in our age of electronic instantaneity, media blitz, and sound bites.

One of the goals of Newspeak is to diminish the value of language by crippling the rich associations of older words and shrinking the size of the vocabulary. Today, evidence of this insidious process is all around us. Newspeak happens when the original meaning of *unique*, "one of a kind," becomes identical with the word *unusual*, as in "That was one of the most unique parties I've ever attended." Newspeak happens when we can no longer distinguish between words such as *uninterested* and *disinterested*, *farther* and *further*, *verbal* and *oral*, *compose* and *comprise*, and *less* and *fewer*. Newspeak happens when we say *momentarily* when we mean *presently* and *presently* when we mean *now*. "We live, man and worm, in a time when almost everything can mean almost anything," wrote humorist James Thurber, whose insights weren't always meant to be humorous.

Another feature of Newspeak is ease of speaking. Words are chosen because they trip so effortlessly off the tongue with a minimum of interference from the mind. As Orwell expresses it, "A Party member called upon to make a political or ethical judgment should be able to spray forth the correct opinions as automatically as a machine gun spraying forth bullets"—a remarkably prescient description of so many political pronouncements of our time.

When a United States senator complains that "the bankers' pockets are bulging with the sweat of the honest working man," when a governor labels his state's budget deficit "an albatross we carry on our back" (which is just as bad as having a monkey around your neck), when an ambassador to the United Nations counsels the Arabs and Israelis to "sit down and settle their differences like good Christian gentlemen," then we have flummoxed, cliché-ridden Newspeak, post-*Nineteen Eighty-Four*.

One group that strives to protect and purify language in the public arena is the Committee on Public Doublespeak, an arm of the National Council of Teachers of English. When it was established in 1973, the Committee took parts of two Orwell coinages, *Doublethink* and *Newspeak*, and combined them to make *Doublespeak*. Doublespeak is language that doesn't call a spade a spade. Rather, Doublespeak calls a spade a heart, or "a manual excavation device." To stanch the spew of Public Doublespeak, the Committee, in its own words, follows "George Orwell's intention of exposing inhumane, propagandistic uses of language . . . with pernicious social or political consequences."

In "Politics and the English Language" Orwell prophesied the coming of Doublespeak when he wrote, "Political language—and with variations this is true of all political parties, from Conservatives to Anarchists—is designed to make lies truthful and murder respectable, and to give an appearance of solidity to pure wind":

> In our time, political speech and writing are largely the defence of the indefensible. Things like the continuance of British rule in India, the Russian purges and deportations, the dropping of the atom bombs on Japan, can indeed be defended, but only by arguments which are too brutal for most people to face, and which do not square with the professed aims of political parties. Thus, political language has to consist largely of euphemism, question-begging and sheer cloudy vagueness. Defenceless villages are bombarded from the air, the inhabitants driven out into the countryside, the cattle machine-gunned, the huts set on fire with incendiary bullets: this is called *pacification*. Millions of peasants are robbed of their farms and sent trudging along the roads with no more than they can carry: this is called *transfer of populations* or *rectification of frontiers*. People are imprisoned for years without trial, or shot in the back of the neck or to die of scurvy in Arctic lumber camps: this is called *elimination of unreliable elements*.

Does this sound like the shrill cry of an over-wrought alarmist? Consider a small sample from among the thousands of specimens of Doublespeak that the NCTE Committee has captured and identified since 1984. They are all real; none has been made up:

• Workers are no longer fired. Instead, they are "reclassified," "deselected," "outplaced," "nonretained," or "nonpositively terminated."

• Recent administrations have never proposed any new taxes, just "revenue enhancement" through new "user's fees."

• United States forces did not invade Grenada. Instead, they executed a "pre-dawn vertical insertion."

• No one died in the student protests in Tiananmen Square. According to Chinese officials, "There was no such thing as bloodshed on Tiananmen Square. It is not from any instance from the soldiers directing their guns at the people. This incident never happened within the area of Beijing."

• In Iraq and Kuwait, hostages and human shields were "foreign guests" cared for by their Iraqi "hosts."

Rather than being a pessimistic determinist, George Orwell was a committed humanist concerned that we not make our ultimate home on an anthill. More powerfully than any other writer, he warned us that dishonest language is a drug that can put conscience to sleep. He set an alarm in our brains to go off when a president names the latest thing in nuclear missiles the Peacekeeper. He helped us to know that when prior public statements are labeled "inoperative," what is really meant is "Don't believe what I told you then. Believe what I tell you now"—and "I lied." He alerted us that when words are used to lie rather than to tell the truth, the house of language grows dark and the human spirit withers.

IV

WRITE ON!

BOOKMOBILITY

It was a dark and stormy night. The wind whistled and the snow swirled as I drove my daughter Katy to junior high school for the dress rehearsal of the seventh-grade play. When we arrived, I decided to wait and retired to the school cafeteria to read a stack of student essays from my eleventh-grade English classes.

Soon after I had hunkered down to my task, three blue-uniformed custodians entered the cafeteria and began sweeping and mopping. No shrinking violet, I was soon engaged in a friendly conversation with one of the men, a burly, lively fellow named Billy. He told me that he was a native son of Concord and that, immediately after graduating from Concord High School, he had gone to work as a printing-machine operator for a large local press. Along with the two other men in the cafeteria, he had recently been laid off by the company.

"So, Dick. I put in twenty-nine years as a printer," Billy explained, "and here I am pushing a mop in a cafeteria."

Then my new friend told me that he could find no printing work north of Boston and that he had been offered a job at one of the local convenience stores where his mother worked, but had decided not to take it. "Why didn't you go to work at the market?" I asked Billy.

A gleam came into his eyes and, pointing a finger at me, he answered: "I'll tell you why, Dick. At a place like that you stand behind a counter for hours, and finally some guy comes in and buys a sandwich. And you know what he does the next day? He s—s it out. But let me tell you, man. I was a maker of books—and people don't s— them out."

Now there, I thought to myself, is a perfect definition of literature—"that which you do not s— out."

My friend at the junior high school cafeteria is not the only person to speak or write eloquently about the staying power of books. "The strongest memory is weaker than the palest ink," says a Chinese proverb. Anatole Broyard tells us, "A good book is never exhausted. It goes on whispering to you from the wall"; Edward Bulwer-Lytton, "Laws die; books never"; and Franklin Roosevelt, "People die, but books never die. No man and no force can abolish memory."

Books live. Books endure and prevail. Not long ago, a woman telephoned an Atlanta library and asked, "Can you please tell me where Scarlett O'Hara is buried?"

The librarian explained, "Scarlett O'Hara is a fictional character in Margaret Mitchell's *Gone With the Wind*."

"Never mind that," said the caller. "I want to know where she's buried."

For that reader, Scarlett O'Hara had been so alive that she was dead.

Books move. Books do not sit still. The first bookmobile in the United States, a horse-drawn wagon operated by a county library in Hagerstown, Maryland, began making its rounds in 1905. But the first bookmobile in history was, perhaps, the property of the Dutch humanist writer Desiderius Erasmus, who wrote the first best-seller, *In Praise of Folly*. Erasmus had few personal possessions outside of his books, and he declared: "When I get a little money, I buy books; and if any is left, I buy food and clothes. My luggage is my library. My home is where my books are." No surprise then that in Erasmus's caravan during his travels throughout sixteenth-century Europe, one donkey was reserved exclusively to carry his books.

Books are not just inert objects to be used for a brief while and returned to the shelf. Like Erasmus, true bibliophiles carry their libraries around with them wherever they go. Emily Dickinson, who went on expeditions everywhere while she stayed at home, knew that bookmobility travels two ways, that our books also take us with them:

> There is no Frigate like a Book
>   To take us Lands away
> Nor any Coursers like a Page
>   Of Prancing Poetry.

> This Traverse may the poorest take
>   Without oppress of Toll—
> How frugal is the Chariot
>   That bears the Human Soul.

To commemorate all those good trips you have taken with books, and all the fascinating journeys to come, I offer my favorite bookish quotations:

• Some books are to be tasted, others to be swallowed, and a few to be chewed and digested.—*Francis Bacon*

• To read without reflecting is like eating without digesting.—*Edmund Burke*

• When you reread a classic, you do not see more in the book than you did before; you see more in *you* than was there before.—*Clifton Fadiman*

• A classic is a book that has never finished saying what it has to say.—*Italo Calvino*

• Farther than arrows, higher than wings fly poet's song and prophet's words.—*Inscription on the Brooklyn Public Library*

• Millions of Americans are not illiterate; they are simply not literate. In other words, they can read and write enough to get by—barely. So they attempt to skim through life by relying on telephones, watching television, or listening to the radio—*Les Trautmann*

• The love of learning, the sequestered nooks/All the sweet serenity of books.—*Henry Wadsworth Longfellow*

• A novelist has made a fictional representation of life. In doing so, he has revealed to us more significance, it may be, than he could find in life itself. —*Bernard de Voto*

• Literature is man's exploration of man by artificial light, which is better than natural light because we can direct it where we want.—*David Daiches*

• As good almost kill a man as kill a good book: who kills a man kills a reasonable creature, God's image; but he who destroys a good book kills reason itself.—*John Milton*

• All good books have one thing in common. They are truer than if they had really happened.—*Ernest Hemingway*

• Without books, history is silent, literature dumb, science crippled, thought and speculation at a standstill. Without books, the development of civilization would have been impossible. They are the engines of change, windows on the world, and lighthouses erected in the sea of time. They are companions, teachers, magicians, bankers of the treasure of the mind. Books are humanity in print.—*Barbara Tuchman*

• The things I want to know are in books; my best friend is the man who'll get me a book I ain't read. —*Abraham Lincoln*

• Any kid who has parents who are interested in him and has a houseful of books isn't poor.—*Sam Levenson*

• A room without books is like a body without a soul.—*Cicero*

• If you're going to be a prisoner of your own mind, the least you can do is make sure it's well furnished.—*Peter Ustinov*

• All that mankind has done, thought, gained, or been: it is lying as in magic preservation in the pages of books.—*Thomas Carlyle*

• Books we must have though we lack bread. —*Alice Brotherton*

• The instruction we find in books is like fire. We fetch it from our neighbors, kindle it at home, communicate it to others, and it becomes the property of all.—*Voltaire*

• These are not books, lumps of lifeless paper, but *minds* alive on the shelves. From each of them goes out its own voice . . . and just as the touch of a button on our set will fill the room with music, so by taking down one of these volumes and opening it, one can call into range the voice of a man far distant in time and space, and hear him speaking to us, mind to mind, heart to heart.—*Gilbert Highet*

• Here genius lies enshrined.
Here sleep in silent majesty
The monarchs of the mind.
—*Inscription in the St. Louis Public Library*

• A book is a gift you can open again and again.
—*Garrison Keillor*

• There is more treasure in books than in all the pirates' loot on Treasure Island . . . and best of all, you can enjoy these riches every day of your life.—*Walt Disney*

• As addictions go, reading is among the cleanest, easiest to feed, happiest.—*Joseph Epstein*

• Books are the legacies that a great genius leaves to mankind, which are delivered down from generation to generation, as presents to posterity of those who are yet unborn.—*Joseph Addison*

• Reading is to the mind what exercise is to the body.—*Richard Steele*

• "What shall I do with my books?" was the question; and the answer "Read them" sobered the questioner.

But if you cannot read them, at any rate handle them and, as it were, fondle them. Peer into them. Let them fall open where they will. Read on from the very first sentence that arrests the eye. Then turn to another. Make a voyage of discovery, taking soundings of uncharted seas. . . . Arrange them on your own plan, so that if you do not know what is in them, you at least know where they are. If they cannot be your friends, let them at any rate be your acquaintances. If they cannot enter the circle of your life, do not deny them at least a nod of recognition.—*Winston Churchill*

• Literature is my Utopia. Here I am not disfranchised. No barrier of the senses shuts me out from the sweet, gracious discourse of my book friends. They talk to me without embarrassment or awkwardness. —*Helen Keller*

• Learning to read . . . we slowly learn to read ourselves. Once we learn how to read, even if then we do not live more wisely, we can at least begin to be aware of why we have not.—*Mark Shorer*

• Some books are undeservedly forgotten, none are undeservedly remembered.—*W. H. Auden*

• Books are the quietest and most constant of friends. They are the most accessible and wisest of counselors, the most patient teachers.—*Charles Eliot*

• A book is the only place in which you can examine a fragile thought without breaking it, or explore an explosive idea without fear that it will go off in your face. . . . It is one of the few havens remaining where a man's mind can get both provocation and privacy.—*Edward P. Morgan*

• A good book is the precious life-blood of a master spirit, imbalm'd and treasur'd up on purpose to a life beyond life.—*Inscription in the New York Public Library*

• A book in the hand is worth two on the shelf. —*Henry T. Coutts*

• The oldest books are still only just out to those who have not read them.—*Samuel Butler*

• The reading of all good books is like conversation with the finest men of past centuries.—*René Descartes*

• Books are the treasured wealth of the world, to

fit the inheritance of generations.—*Henry David Thoreau*

• Read the best books first, or you may not have a chance to read them at all.—*Henry David Thoreau*

• How many a man has dated a new era in his life from the reading of a book!—*Henry David Thoreau*

• A book ought to be an icepick to break up the frozen sea within us.—*Franz Kafka*

• There is hardly any grief that an hour's reading will not dissipate.—*Montesquieu*

• The pleasure of all reading is doubled when one lives with another who shares the same books. —*Katherine Mansfield*

• Just the knowledge that a good book is awaiting one at the end of a long day makes that day happier. —*Kathleen Norris*

• Every man who knows how to read has it in him power to magnify himself, to multiply the ways in which he exists, to make his life full, significant, and interesting.—*Aldous Huxley*

• It is not true that we have only one life to live; if we can read, we can live as many more lives and kinds of lives as we wish.—*S. I. Hayakawa*

• The greatest gift is the passion for reading. It is cheap, it consoles, it distracts, it excites, it gives you moral knowledge of the world and experience of a wide kind. It is moral illumination.—*Elizabeth Hardwick*

• I am part of all that I have read.—*John Kieran*

• What is a book? Part matter and part spirit; part thing and part thought—however you look at it, it defies definition.—*Ernest O. Hauser*

• Books are more than books. They are the life, the very heart and core of ages past, the reason why men lived and worked and died, the essence and quintessence of their lives.—*Amy Lowell*

• The writings of the wise are the only riches our posterity cannot squander.—*Lander*

• Books are the most enduring monument of man's achievement. Through them, civilization becomes cumulative.—*Inscription in the Detroit Public Library*

• There are no bad books any more than there are ugly women.—*Anatole France*

• The information I most want is in books not yet written by people not yet born.—*Ashleigh Brilliant*

• A book is like a garden carried in the pocket. —*Chinese proverb*

A CELEBRATION
OF LIBRARIES

Just about everyone has seen the blue highway signs with the big white *H* and an arrow pointing the way to the nearest hospital. Some state library associations have suggested that our roads be fringed by a similar kind of road marker with a prominently displayed *L* and an arrow pointing in the direction of another local institution: the public library. Such a sign would remind us that librarians serve us in much the same way as doctors and nurses and that books are just as vital to our health as bandages and medicine.

Elinor Lander Horwitz once wrote in *The Washington Post*, "There are numerous men and women perambulating the earth—in appearance much like ordinary respectable citizens—who have warm, loving, passionate—even sensuous—feelings about libraries."

After I published a column tracing the history of libraries in the United States, Gertrude King Ramstrom, of Nashua, New Hampshire, sent me her "warm, loving, passionate—even sensuous—feelings" about her childhood adventures in a New England town library. Her testimonial makes vivid Shakespeare's claim that "my library was dukedom large enough."

Dear Sir:

Your article about libraries whisked me back in time and place to the 1920s and the little village of Haydenville, Massachusetts, where I grew up. Its tiny library, which is still in use, was our only avenue of adventure to the wonders of the outside world, and my brothers and I, along with our friends, made good use of it.

It is not a very imposing building either in architecture or size, and a traveler probably would not even realize one was there. Although it is on Main Street, it is tucked back at an angle to the road and has a mien of withdrawal, or shyness, as if aware of its insignificance among the libraries of the world. But to us it was a structure of great importance.

Its single room is shaped like the letter *H* with the crosspiece widened to include almost the entire area. Wonderful little nooks, furnished with stools and chairs, are formed by the extensions of the vertical bars of the *H*, and that was where we acquired a glimpse of the world, had our curiosity aroused, and met with our friends. It was open every Friday evening, and directly after supper Mother made us wash up and comb our hair so we would look respectable and be clean enough to inspect books without leaving fingerprints. Most of our friends were doing the same, and about 7 P.M. we congregated on the wide stone step of the building.

On summer evenings we lingered outside to talk, but in winter it was nice to push into the room and stand over the one-pipe register and allow the heat to blow up around us. There were no rules about talking, except when we became too boisterous, so the boys jostled and joked in one nook while we girls squeezed into another to whisper and giggle.

In our little library was born my love of history, which became my major in college. From *The Colonial Twins*, *The Puritan Twins*, and *The Twins of the American Revolution* through *The Red Badge of Courage* and *With Malice Toward None* I read, and am still reading, every historical novel available. By corroborating their assertions with the facts of history, I have found a never-ending source of enlightenment.

While my brothers read *The Bobbsey Twins*, *Tom Swift*, and *Huck Finn*, I read *Pollyanna*, *Bambi*, and *The Yearling*. As we grew, my older brother turned to *Twenty Thousand Leagues Under the Sea* and almost wore out Lindbergh's *We*. I can still picture the blue binding of the book with a silver airplane etched on the cover and my brother slouched in a big easy chair with his leg dangling over its arm. Both socks wrinkled around his ankles showing bare legs below the cuffs of his knicker pants, and his hand rumpled his hair as he soared high over the earth with his hero.

As he traveled the skies and seas, I traversed America with Willa Cather, learned to love animals through Albert Payson Terhune stories, found goodness in life with A. J. Cronin, and whisked away on the whimsy of Elizabeth Goudge. It was a wonderful experience, and because of it I would add another beatitude to the ones we learned back in our Sunday School days: Blessed are they who can read and enjoy a good book for theirs is the world and its kingdoms.

I firmly believe that children are influenced by what they read and that the books we took home from the library impressed upon us what Mother and Dad tried to teach—that good character and high moral values are to be desired above all other attributes. We heard it, we read it, and so we lived it. There is no greater endowment that can be given a child than an ideal and a hero, and our little library did just that for us.

Gertrude Ramstrom's paean inspires me to share a dozen of my favorite quotable quotations about libraries:

• Libraries are user-friendly.—*American Library Association*

• A library implies an act of faith which generations, still in darkness hid, sign in their night in witness of the dawn.—*Victor Hugo*

• I have always imagined that Paradise will be a kind of library!—*John Cheever*

• Take one brisk walk to the library. Take out any book by a tried-and-true writer. Take a brisk walk home and read with all attention. The exercise plus the tonic of the book will provide all physical and mental requirements for good health.—*Helen Hayes, at age eighty-six*

• I am a self-confessed library buff, drawn to them like others are drawn to theaters, art galleries, bars, or football games. I am proud to say that I have more library cards than credit cards in my wallet and that I know where all the coffee machines are located at the Library of Congress.—*Paul Dickson*

• Libraries will get you through times of no money better than money will get you through times of no libraries.—*Library poster*

• Perhaps no place in any community is so totally democratic as the town library. The only entrance requirement is interest.—*Lady Bird Johnson*

• In an era when millions more Americans can identify Boy George than George Eliot, it is gratifying to know that there is still a place where making acquaintance with Eliot and other literary giants is as easy as a walk or a drive to that spectacular intellectual galaxy, the local public library.—*Michael Birkner*

• Call it impiety, but to me the very word *library* has a sanctity that *church* cannot gain. The sacredness is my own association, of course. It is thick walls and tall windows. It is quiet rustling pages that whisper of knowledge. It is cool and smelly with that exciting odor that can only be got from aging glue, printers ink, paper, leather, and ideas together.—*A. C. Greene*

• A great library contains the diary of the human race.—*George Dawson*

• Libraries remain the meccas of self-help, the most open of open universities . . . where there are no entrance examinations and no diplomas, and where one can enter at any age.—*Daniel J. Boorstin*

• In a library it's hard to avoid reading.—*From a student essay*

YA GOT ANY GOOD BOOKS HERE?

"**D**ear Mr. Lederer," wrote Lorraine Stickney, a librarian at Gorham High School in Gorham, Maine, "I have been enjoying your column for a long time, and it occurred to me that you might gain some similar enjoyment from the enclosed material. These are comments, questions, and requests we have received in the Gorham High School Library over the years. Some you may find quite humorous, even though they may not have intended to be so."

What Lorraine Stickney sent me were twenty sheets entitled "An Average Day in the Life of the Gorham High School Library" that, taken together, offer revealing insights into what it is like to be a school librarian. Here are the brightest of the gems:

- Ya got any good books here?
- Have you got that article I wanted to read? I don't remember what it was or what magazine it was in.

- I lost my English book. Where did it go?
- Have you got any paper clips?
- Do you have any books about people who get wiped out or mangled?
- Do you have the book of Genesis? You know, it tells about the woman with the smallest waist and things like that. [The student means the *Guinness Book of World Records*.]
- Can I get a social security card here?
- I can't read this book. The words are too tiny.
- Who was that Greek guy, the only place you could kill him was in the heel?
- Do you know anything about the United States?
- Do you have any alcohol? My ears are pierced and they're killing me!
- I need to find the Loch Ness Monster. What do you have?
- Where are your hysterical novels?
- Do you have any string? Well, buy some.
- I came in to look up the word *kleptomaniac*, but someone has stolen all the dictionaries.
- Can you find me a recipe for Jewish unleavened bread?
- Are we supposed to get new library cards for this month, or is it still last month?
- Do you have any pornographic books?
- Do you have a rubber thumb we could borrow?
- I need an ancient current event.
- What do you call a person who eats only vegetables? I think it starts with a *v*.
- Ya got anything I can report on?
- I just read *Midnight Summer Dream*. Do you have another play by Shakespeare?
- Would you give me a back rub?

- Who were the Seven Dwarfs?
- Do you have a brown button I could borrow?
- What are the Maine state laws regarding nudity? Is nudity allowed in national parks?
- Where can I find instructions for brewing my own beer?
- Do you have anything to read in this place?
- Did I bring that book back?
- What was a chastity belt used for?
- Are ladies of the night the same as ladies of the evening?
- I've got a report due next period. What can I do it on?
- Do you have a razor blade and a bucket?
- I need an American classic. Not too long, but at least 173 pages.
- Do you have a picture of Lenin under glass?
- May I put this projector in the I.V. room?
- I need a book by Tom Sawyer.
- Do you have a postal service here? Do you have a stamp?
- What's the easiest animal to report on?
- Does a chicken have a vagina?
- Do you have a three-ringed hole-poker?
- How do you know when you die?
- Do you have a photograph of the devil?
- Do you have a copy of *The Canterbur* written in our language?
- Do you have the book *Pardon Me,* *ping on My Eyeball?*
- What's a good disease?
- Where is the Panama Cana
- Is Europe in America? W
- May I have some yell

- What do you call those things that you put at the bottom of paper? Are they feetnotes?
- I want a book with no chapters. Chapters bug me.
- Haven't you got something easier than this book? This must have at least a thousand words in it.
- Do you have a photograph of a dragon?
- What date is New Year's Eve?
- Were Mary and Joseph married when Jesus was born? How about when he was conceived? Did they even know each other? It says here, "And he knew her not."
- How do I find a book that I don't remember the name of?

What was it about?

I don't remember, but it was orange.

Blessed be our school librarians. Amalgams of scholars, teachers, counselors, traffic controllers, and baby-sitters, they march in the company of secular saints. May their tribe thrive and multiply.

WHAT IS POETRY?

Whenever my friend and St. Paul's School colleague Larry Katzenbach teaches poetry to his English classes, he begins with a story, one that starts out long ago, perhaps 140 million years in the past, and maybe more. The story is about a great gray dinosaur, and it starts sadly, with that dinosaur dying, sinking into the black mud in which he had been wallowing and being covered by shreds of leaf, bark, and root—all the dark debris that had been his life.

Many ages passed, millions of years, and the muck about the dinosaur's body hardened and fossilized. Pressures built, and the gray beast took on the black of the soil enwrapping it, and the dark remains became compressed. Gradually, ever so slowly, the creature turned into coal. More eons elapsed and more weight pressed down upon the coal, until, deep in the earth, beneath layers and layers of history, the dinosaur became a diamond.

That is all we have left of the great beast, and yet

the story has ended happily. For in that diamond's glittering facets are the compacted memories of all the time that has passed between the long-ago dinosaur and us, who today marvel at the diamond's brilliant whiteness and who listen to this story.

Poems are life transmuted into diamonds, compact and indestructible. To some of us today, poetry may seem an artificial refinement of natural speech. But in the literature of every country, poetry comes before prose. "Poetry is the eldest sister of all arts, and parent to most," according to the playwright William Congreve. It is the oldest language we have—the most primitive, the most elemental, and the most natural expression of ourselves as human beings. Poet John Frederick Nims has said that "poetry is the way it is because we are the way we are."

"I could no more define poetry than a terrier can define a rat," observes the English poet A. E. Housman. It is doubtful that words can ever bottle the full essence of poetry, and fabricating a definition of poetry to fit every poem may be as baggy and rumpled as a suit to fit every man. As Dylan Thomas cautions about such attempts, "There is no such thing as poetry, only poems." Still, the following anthology of statements may help to broaden our understanding of what it is poetry tries to do:

• Language is the greatest achievement of culture; poetry is the greatest achievement of language. —*Vladimir Alexandrov*

• The magic of literary art, especially poetry, consists in suggesting with words what words cannot possibly say.—*Martin Angoff*

• Poetry is simply the most beautiful, impressive,

and widely effective mode of saying things.—*Matthew Arnold*

• To write poetry, I must soak myself with the gasoline of words and then torch myself so that I can burn bright and see what's going on around me. Writing poetry, that act of language and fire, makes me feel purpose in a universe that often feels like a severe joke.—*Michael Bettencourt*

• That the poems are useful to other people, that they are bread, that they can be eaten, and strengthen strangers, that is precisely our goal, our reward, our vocation.—*Robert Bly*

• At certain periods of history it is only poetry that is capable of dealing with reality by condensing it into something graspable, something that otherwise wouldn't be retained by the mind.—*Joseph Brodsky*

• Poetry is one of the forms of joy, the most articulate, the most expanding, and, therefore, the most fulfilling form. It is no separation from the world; it is the mankind of the world, the most human language of man's uncertain romance with the universe.—*John Ciardi*

• The poet is a liar who always speaks the truth. —*Jean Cocteau*

• If I read a book, and it makes my body so cold no fire can ever warm me, I know *that* is poetry. If I feel physically as if the top of my head were taken off, I know *that* is poetry. These are the only ways I know it. Is there any other way?—*Emily Dickinson*

• A poem is a momentary stay against confusion.—*Robert Frost*

• Poetry is the language in which man explores his own amazement.—*Christopher Fry*

- Poetry is truth dwelling in beauty.—*Gilfillan*
- There is no money in poetry, but then there is no poetry in money, either.—*Robert Graves*
- Poetry is the art of uniting pleasure with truth.—*Samuel Johnson*
- When power leads man to arrogance, poetry reminds him of his limitations. When power narrows the area of man's concern, poetry reminds him of the richness and diversity of his existence. When power corrupts, poetry cleanses.—*John F. Kennedy*
- Poetry is something to care about. In fact, a persuasion of long standing among mankind is that the hearing of a poem, as well as the making of a poem, is nothing less than a religious act. Poetry, in speech and song, was inseparable from classic Greek drama, which—for playwright, actor, and spectator alike—was a holy-day ceremony.—*X. J. Kennedy*
- A poem should not mean/But be.—*Archibald Macleish*
- The crown of literature is poetry. It is its end and aim. It is the sublimest activity of the human mind. It is the achievement of beauty and delicacy. The writer of prose can only step aside when the poet passes.—*W. Somerset Maugham*
- Poetry is fact given over to imagery.—*Rod McKuen*
- Poetry might be defined as a kind of language that says more and says it more intensely than does ordinary language.—*Laurence Perrine*
- Poetry is news that is still news.—*Ezra Pound*
- Poetry is the synthesis of hyacinths and biscuits.—*Carl Sandburg*
- Something well said is something well said, but something superbly said is a poem.—*Lewis Putnam Turco*

• Poetry is the power of defining the indefinable in terms of the unforgettable.—*Louis Untermeyer*

• One merit of poetry few people will deny: it says more and in fewer words than does prose. —*Voltaire*

• A poem compresses much into a small space and adds music, thus heightening its meaning.—*E. B. White*

• Poetry is the spontaneous overflow of powerful feelings: it takes its origin from emotion recollected in tranquillity.—*William Wordsworth*

• God guard me from the thoughts men think
  In the mind alone.
  He that sings a lasting song
  Thinks in a marrow bone.

                              —*William Butler Yeats*

YOU CAN BE
A POET

In "I Taste a Liquor Never Brewed," Emily Dickinson expresses her intoxication with poetry:

> I taste a liquor never brewed—
> From Tankards scooped in Pearl—
> Not all the vats upon the Rhine
> Yield such an Alcohol!
>
> Inebriate of Air—am I—
> And Debauchee of Dew—
> Reeling—thro endless summer days—
> From inns of Molten Blue.

While you may never have gotten drunk on poetry, chances are that you have sipped it from time to time. And if the magic and music of the poems have done their work upon you, you have come to see that poetry is a form of expression more concise and concentrated than prose, that the language of poetry exerts a greater pressure per square syllable and a greater intensity per word than any other form of communication.

I invite you to try your hand, mind, and heart at writing poetry yourself. Even if you have never created a poem before, you may have sensed that a poem is lurking somewhere inside you, that among the many experiences in your life are some that can best be told in the special language and form of poetry.

A poem "begins in delight and ends in wisdom," Robert Frost tells us in his delightful and wise essay "The Figure a Poem Makes." Writing poetry can help you to become more aware of your experiences and to bring into focus thoughts that might otherwise seem jumbled and unrelated. Making your own poems can also help you to appreciate poetry more authentically by encouraging you to see that all human beings are, in their own way, poets. As an ancient Chinese proverb says, "Tell me, I forget. Show me, I remember. Involve me, I understand."

Henry David Thoreau contends that "the one great rule of composition is to speak the truth." To broadcast truth in your poetry, you must write about events and perceptions that grow out of your life and genuinely interest you. One misconception about poetry is that it is devoted exclusively to lofty themes like immortality and unrequited love or to a small group of poetic subjects like clouds and daffodils. In fact, poetry takes all life as its province. A poem can talk about anything—the strange and the common, the beautiful and the ugly, the ideal and the mundane—as long as the poet and the reader will care about it.

The place to begin is with yourself. If your poems are to be sincere, they should be fashioned from the raw material of your experience, whether that material be cars or computers, surfing or sewing, family or friends, city or country.

Nobody can tell you what to say. What follows are suggestions for saying it. At its heart, poetry is a meeting of elemental experiences with elemental forms. Experimenting with various forms of poetry may help you to narrow the gap over which the spark of creation must leap.

Poets are collectors—of words, of images, of memories, of experiences. Sometimes a collection of related ideas naturally gathers itself into a poem that is very like a list. Make a list of things that make you feel warm, sounds you hear at night, qualities of things you like a lot, objects that are your favorite color.

Let the ideas flow, one after the other, one into the other. Don't worry about rhythm or meter. Create a list in which each line or grouping of lines begins with a repeated expression—"I wish that . . . ," "I dreamed that . . . ," "I seem to be . . ./But I really am . . ." Now transform your list of impressions and images into a free-flowing poem.

Experience comes to us largely through the senses, and poetry, like life itself, is generally filled with sensory details, called imagery. Though the term *image* suggests something that is seen, an image is a word or sequence of words that evokes a picture, a sound, a taste, a smell, or a touch.

The eighteenth-century Japanese poet Tanaguchi Buson wrote a poem on the death of his beloved wife. Had he wished, Buson could have written an essay about the dead woman, contrasting her death and her life or stating his feelings about the terror of death in general. Instead he wrote a haiku:

The piercing chill I feel:
My dead wife's comb in our bedroom,
Under my heel.

Striking his bare foot against the comb, cold and motionless but so associated with the living woman who had worn it in her hair, the widower (and the reader) feels the shock as if he had touched the dead woman's corpse. Rather than abstractly expostulating upon his wife's death, the poet has evoked a sympathetic tingling of the nerve ends, from the foot right up to the heart and brain.

Try writing a few poems in the form of the time-honored haiku. The haiku is a traditional form of Japanese verse fashioned from three short lines of five, seven, and five syllables respectively, a total of seventeen syllables in all. We can appreciate the conciseness of the haiku form by realizing that we can normally utter about seventeen syllables with a single breath. (Note: Buson's poem conforms to the five-seven-five pattern in the original Japanese but varies slightly in the English translation. In some haiku the first and third lines rhyme; in others they don't.)

The heart of the haiku poem is its imagery. A haiku doesn't philosophize about life. Rather, it beckons the reader to enter directly into the poet's experience through the door of the senses. Thus, in your haiku create a single, vivid image that will invite your readers to grasp the idea in concrete terms, as in these examples from my tenth-grade students:

Youth plays forever:
A little child hides behind
A crumbling tombstone.

She, almost alone:
A jitterbugging feather
Bows and dances by.

Megalopolis:
A little man watering
A dried blade of grass.

Now it's time to do some figurative speaking in your poetry.

In contrast to literal language, which is basically factual, figurative language tells it like it isn't to show the way it really is. The most pervasive of all figures of speech is the metaphor (the word originally meant "carry beyond"), a comparison of two objects or ideas that are not alike in a literal sense but can be fused imaginatively (figuratively) in the reader's mind.

One of the most famous metaphors in modern poetry occurs in T. S. Eliot's "The Love-Song of J. Alfred Prufrock" when the hollow, ineffective Mr. Prufrock laments, "I have measured out my life in coffee spoons." Eliot did not mean that Prufrock literally spooned out his days from a coffee can, but in creating his metaphor the poet telescoped two suggestions into one: that of partaking of life in tiny sips instead of savoring it fully and that of spacing life out in superficial parties.

Emerging one day from a train in the Paris subway, Eliot's mentor, Ezra Pound, beheld "suddenly a beautiful face, and another and another." Originally he described his impression in a poem thirty lines long, but his final version was a metaphor of but two lines:

The apparition of these faces in the crowd;
Petals on a wet, black bough.

Within the brief compass of two lines, Pound caught and crystallized his moment of awareness and transmitted it for others to enjoy. By writing Ezra Pound couplets, as they are called, you too can create vivid metaphors and speak to other human beings, as have my sophomore students:

A child in the slums;
A withered flower in a dusty birdbath.

Winter poplars gaunt and straight;
Old brooms in a witch's cupboard.

A dogwood blooming petals in spring;
Cinderella granted her gown for the ball.

In his famous couplet, Ezra Pound located the first half of his metaphor in the first line and the second half in the second line. In "A Noiseless Patient Spider," Walt Whitman devoted a full free-verse stanza to each half of his metaphor, comparing a spider (first stanza) and a human soul (second stanza) as entities that each seek a reference point upon which to build an existence. Whitman was a master of free verse, a form that Laurence Peter has called "the triumph of mind over meter." Free verse eschews regular meter and rhyme and relies upon the natural speech rhythms of language and the mellifluous cadences formed by stressed and unstressed syllables. Read "A Noiseless Patient Spider" aloud and listen to the easy music of its rhythms:

A noiseless patient spider,
I mark'd where on a little promontory
   it stood isolated,
Mark'd how to explore
   the vacant vast surroundings,
It launch'd forth filament, filament, filament,
   out of itself,
Ever unreeling them, ever tirelessly speeding them.

And you O my soul where you stand,
Surrounded, detached, in measureless oceans of space,
Ceaselessly musing, venturing, throwing,
   seeking the spheres to connect them,
Till the bridge you will need be form'd,
   till the ductile anchor hold,
Till the gossamer thread you fling catch somewhere,
   O my soul.

Choose two ideas or objects that are not ordinarily associated with each other and, in a single sentence, state their crucial point of similarity. Then, using Whitman's spider poem as a model, create a free-verse poem that develops the two hemispheres of your metaphor, as in this student example:

A butterfly, alone in its timeless world.
It does not hear the rumble and squawk of the cars.
It does not smell the smoke and waste of the city.
It seeks out only trees and flowers
And is content to be a part of them.

My child plays on her swing,
Laughing as she rocks to and from the earth.
She does not see the broken pavements
And the patches of weeds blasting through the earth.

She only sees her tiny feet
Kicking towards the sun.

—*Ashley Elinor*

In the comic strip "B.C." a mangy bird occasionally poses riddles to a tortoise on whose shell he is perched. In one sequence of panels, the bird asks, "What goes: hornge, mornge, gornge, flornge, scornge aarrgghhh!?"

"Beats me, what?" sighs the tortoise.

And the bird answers: "A poet trying to rhyme 'orange.' "

Rhyme is the repetition of accented vowel sounds and all succeeding sounds—*walk* and *talk*, *simple* and *pimple*, *minister* and *sinister*. Many a poem has been ruined by misguided attempts to force words to rhyme (alas, there is no natural common word that rhymes with *orange*), but many another has gained power and been made more memorable by the pleasing repetition of rhyming words.

Another vital element in the melody of poetic language is meter, the arrangement of sounds into a pattern of stressed and unstressed syllables. Laurence Perrine identifies meter as "the kind of rhythm we can tap our foot to." In fact, the basic metrical unit is called a foot and consists of one accented syllable plus one or two unaccented syllables:

Example	Name of foot	Name of meter
Iráq	iamb	iambic
Éngland	trochee	trochaic
Japanése	anapest	anapestic
Cánada	dactyl	dactylic

The meter of a line is measured by naming the number of feet in it:

one foot: monometer   four feet: tetrameter
two feet: dimeter   five feet: pentameter
three feet: trimeter   six feet: hexameter

Here is a little poem that will help you to remember how to measure meter:

The *íambs* gó from shórt to lóng.—(iambic
    tetrameter)
Tróchees síng a márching sóng.—(trochaic tetrameter)
Dáctyls go dáncing as líght as a féather.—(dactylic
    tetrameter)
But the *ánapest's* dífferent, you sée, altogéther.—
    (anapestic tetrameter)

Show off your abilities as a meter man or meter maid by creating your own rhymed and metered couplets. This activity presents many of the same challenges as writing a longer poem—the dialogue between form and meaning, the fusion of imagination and technical skill.

Each of your couplets should be a self-contained poem that says something witty or wise or beautiful. Within each couplet, lines should be in the same meter and should rhyme truly. Try on various feet for size—iambic, trochaic, anapestic, and dactylic, as in these student couplets:

Long hair is causing such a fit,
But Samson got away with it. (iambic)

Madhouse windows, painted flowered sin;
Star-devouring, shadow inmates grin. (trochaic)

He was ever so handsome and gracefully tall,
But inside of his head was nothing at all. (anapestic)

Grubby gym sneakers lined up in a row:
White-footed centipede giving a show. (dactylic)

For a closing exercise I am going to ask you to go out on a limerick.

Art appeals to our love of pattern, and many poems are shaped into patterns called stanzas. A stanza is a cluster of lines having the same meter and rhyme scheme that is repeated throughout a given poem or that becomes a traditional form in which many poems, over time, are cast.

While other basic forms of poetry, like the sonnet and ode, are borrowed from other countries, the limerick, which takes its name from a county in Ireland, is an original English creation and the most familiar of all traditional verse patterns in our language. It has been estimated that at least a million limericks—good, mediocre, and indelicate—are in existence today. The swift, catchy meter, short lines, and clever rhymes make the limerick stanza particularly suitable for humorous and nonsense verse, so much so that it is impossible to imagine a serious limerick.

By definition, the limerick is a comic poem of five anapestic lines, of which lines one, two, and five have three feet and rhyme, and lines three and four have two feet and rhyme, as in this classic:

There was a young lady quite bright,
Whose speed was much faster than light.

> She set out one day
> In a relative way
> And returned on the previous night.

Join the thousands of limericists who have come before you and take a crack at writing the great American limerick. Using the five-line pattern of the limerick, tell an engaging story or make a humorous statement compactly and cleverly, as in this student example:

> An ugly old hag named Cruella
> Once married a fella named Bela.
> "I really can't gripe,"
> Said she, "He's my type.
> He hangs from the top of the cella."

Not long ago the poet and critic William Meredith said, "I expect that hang-gliding must be like poetry. Once you get used to it, you can't imagine not wanting the scare of it. But it's more serious than hang-gliding. Poetry is the safest known mode of human existence. You only risk staying alive."

Take the risk. If you come to the adventure of writing poetry with an open mind and heart, willing to hear, willing to see, and willing to feel, you will find yourself gliding through an exhilarating journey that begins in delight and ends in wisdom.

A LETTER
IS FOREVER

DAUGHTER [going off to college]: *I'm going to write you every week, Daddy.*
DAD: *Yeh, like when you went away to camp.*
DAUGHTER: *Dad, I really mean it.*
DAD: *You won't write; you'll call. Here's your personal 800 number, and you won't need any money.*
DAUGHTER: *Dad, can I have some money anyway?*

—Telephone company television commercial

In the world today there seems to be a conspiracy against the writing of personal letters. The glut of junk mail makes the arrival of the post a less special and exciting event, and the buzz and bleep and glow of competing media—video games, compact discs, radio, and television—stifle the act of writing itself. Like the mermaids who beckoned Odysseus with the enchantment of their song, the telephone companies entice us to "reach out and touch someone" by pushing a few buttons, speaking through wires, and joining that someone in an instantaneously intimate exchange. The age of speed dialing has so reprogrammed our neurons, it seems, that we can no longer tolerate any gulf between input and response.

In 1979 Postmaster General William F. Bolger wrote to a number of prominent Americans, seeking their comments on the importance of personal correspondence. One response to the postmaster's call came from a famous children's television host who had made bangs popular before the Beatles:

> The telephone, as brilliant an invention as it is, has changed the letter-writing habits of all of us. It's so much easier to pick up the phone than to put pen to paper.
>
> But think of what it means to a grandmother in another city to discover a mailbox with a letter from her granddaughter. For a son away at camp, in the American Forces overseas, or at college, to get a letter from home with some money in it to pay the phone bill. And hopefully by return post, a thank you note to Mom and Dad.
>
> Letters become a part of everyone's personal history and present a side of someone that might be lost otherwise. A phone call is a one-time thing that can't be saved. A letter can last a lifetime.
>
> Captain Kangaroo

There is indeed something special and enduring about a personal letter that allows us to "reach out and touch someone" in a way that a telephone call can't. A letter is an intimation of and invitation to immortality: as long as a letter endures, its writer's thoughts live on. The letters of St. Paul, for example, have lasted almost two thousand years, and the thirteenth chapter of Paul's First Letter to the Corinthians is probably the best-known epistolary passage in our culture:

> And though I have the gift of prophecy, and understand all mysteries, and all knowledge; and though I have all faith, so that I could remove mountains, and have not charity, I am nothing. . . .
>
> When I was a child, I spake as a child, I understood as a child, I thought as a child; but when I became a man, I put away childish things.
>
> For now we see through a glass darkly; but then face to face: now I know in part; but then shall I know even as also I am known.
>
> And now abideth faith, hope, and charity, these three; but the greatest of these is charity.

Next only to conversation, letters are the most universal and personal form of communication in words. You may never become a published author, but one kind of writing is available to you as long as you live. You can write letters.

If you think that you're too busy for personal correspondence, consider the life of our friend Charles Lutwidge Dodgson. In addition to teaching, composing mathematical treatises, fabricating word games, photographing thousands of subjects, and, as Lewis Carroll, writing *Alice in Wonderland*, *Through the Looking Glass*, and *The Hunting of the Snark*, Carroll was a prolific letter writer—perhaps the most fastidious and persistent ever—sometimes producing more than a dozen in a single day and a thousand in a single year. Besides those dealing with business matters, Carroll wrote many social letters to relatives and friends, acknowledging their birthdays, congratulating them on marriages, and thanking them for tea parties or country weekends. During his lifetime he wrote more than one hundred thousand letters, and he cataloged them all.

Or consider President Abraham Lincoln. Was there anyone ever busier than Lincoln, or was there anyone who should have been more oppressed by the weight of grief for an entire people? Even while a sundered nation was slaughtering itself on the battlefields of the Civil War, Lincoln could still find time, on November 21, 1864, to write this letter to Mrs. Bixby:

> Dear Madam:
> I have been shown in the files of the War Department a statement of the Adjutant-General of Massachusetts that you are the mother of five sons who have died gloriously on the field of battle. I feel how weak and fruitless must be any words of mine which should attempt to beguile you from the grief of a loss so overwhelming. But I cannot refrain from tendering to you the consolation that may be found in the thanks of the Republic they died to save. I pray that our Heavenly Father may assuage the anguish of your bereavement, and leave you only the cherished memory of the loved and lost, and the solemn pride that must be yours to have laid so costly a sacrifice upon the altar of freedom.
> Yours very sincerely and respectfully,
>
>   A. Lincoln

Composing a letter invites us to make a point with a clarity of argument and richness of tone not easily achieved with oral communication. Letter-writing releases us from the tyranny of the present and gives us time to think. Unlike a telephone conversation, which requires instant give and take, putting ourselves on paper allows us to take time to say, without interruption, exactly what we mean, to establish a private space between impulse and statement. Because we can't take back a letter in the same way we can instantly retract an oral statement, letters demand forethought, organization, and a high degree of sincerity.

On June 17, 1774, the commissioners from Maryland and Virginia negotiated a treaty with the Native Americans of the Six Nations at Lancaster, Pennsylvania. To an invitation that they send their sons to William and Mary College the tribal members replied:

> We know that you highly esteem the kind of Learning taught in those Colleges, and that the Maintenance of our young Men, while with you, would be very expensive to you. We are convinced that you mean to do us Good by your Proposal; and we thank you heartily.

> But you, who are wise, must know that different Nations have different Conceptions of things and you will therefore not take it amiss, if our ideas of this kind of Education happen not to be the same as yours. We have had some experience with it. Several of our young People were formerly brought up at the Colleges of the Northern provinces: they were instructed in all your Sciences; but, when they came back to us, they were bad Runners, ignorant of every means of living in the

woods . . . neither fit for hunters, Warriors, nor Counsellors, they were totally good for nothing.

We are, however, not the less oblig'd by your kind Offer, tho' we decline accepting it; and, to show our grateful Sense of it, if the Gentlemen of Virginia will send us a Dozen of their Sons, we will take Care of their Education, instruct them in all we know, and make Men of them.

When, in 1885, Mark Twain's *The Adventures of Huckleberry Finn* was published in the United States, a number of influential reviewers lambasted the book for its low characters, language, and taste. The cruelest blow of all was dealt by the Public Library Committee of Concord, Massachusetts, which banned *Huckleberry Finn* from the library shelves on the grounds that it depicted "a series of experiences not elevating." When, shortly thereafter, the Free Trade Club of Concord offered Twain an honorary membership, the author saw his chance to strike back at the Library Committee by writing this letter to the Secretary of the Free Trade Club:

> Dear Sir—
> . . . It does look as if Massachusetts were in a fair way to embarrass me with kindness this year. . . . A committee of the public library of your own town has condemned and excommunicated my last book and doubled its sale. This generous action of theirs must necessarily benefit me in one or two additional ways. For instance, it will deter other libraries from buying the book; and you are doubtless aware that one book in a public library prevents the sale of a sure ten and a possible hundred of its mates. And secondly it will

cause the purchasers of the book to read it, out of curiosity, instead of merely intending to do so after the usual way of the world and library committees; and then they will discover, to my great advantage and their own indignant disappointment, that there is nothing objectionable in the book, after all.

And finally, the Free Trade Club of Concord comes forward and adds to the splendid burden of obligations already conferred upon me by the Commonwealth of Massachusetts an honorary membership which is more worth than all the rest, just at this juncture, since it endorses me as worthy to associate with gentlemen whom even the moral icebergs of the Concord library committee are bound to respect.

May the great Commonwealth of Massachusetts endure forever, is the heartfelt prayer of one who, long a recipient of her mere general good will, is proud to realize that he is at last become her pet.

Between 1872 and 1890, the Dutch expressionist painter Vincent Van Gogh wrote hundreds of letters to his younger brother, Theo. In this exchange between two affectionate brothers, Van Gogh shows a remarkable ability to paint with words and to employ words to talk about his painting:

> Mysteries remain, and sorrow or melancholy, but that eternal negative is balanced by the positive work which is thus achieved after all. If life were as simple, and things as little complicated by a goody-goody's story or the hackneyed sermon of the average clergyman, it wouldn't be so very difficult to make one's way. But it isn't, and things are infinitely more complicated, and right and wrong do not exist separately,

any more than black and white do in nature. One must be careful not to fall back on opaque black—on deliberate wrong—and even more, one has to avoid the white as of a whitewashed wall, which means hypocrisy and everlasting Pharisaism. He who courageously tries to follow his reason, and especially his conscience, the very highest reason—the sublime reason—and tries to stay honest, can hardly lose his way entirely, I think, though he will not get off without mistakes, rebuffs, and moments of weakness, and will not achieve perfection.

Near the end of his life, Van Gogh was admitted to the asylum at Saint-Remy, where he was smitten by terrible seizures. Of one of these he wrote his brother: "My work was going well, the last canvas of branches in blossom—you will see that it was perhaps the best, the most patiently worked thing I had done, painted with calm and with greater firmness of touch. And the next day, down like a brute. Difficult to understand things like that, but alas! it's like that."

Even as he was descending into madness, Van Gogh, on April 15, 1890, near the end of his life, sent his brother a note of concern and comfort:

Today I wanted to read the letters which had come for me, but I was not clear-headed enough to be able to understand them. However, I am trying to answer you at once, and I hope that this [attack] will clear in a few days. Above all I hope that you are well, and your wife and child too. Don't worry about me, even if this should last a bit longer, and write the same thing to those at home and give them kindest regards from me. . . .

My poor boy, just take things as they come, don't be grieved over me, it will encourage and sustain me more than you think, to know that you are running your household well. Then after a time of affliction perhaps peaceful days will come again for me too.

Vincent died on July 30, 1890. Just a few weeks before, he was able to write, "I still love art and life very much indeed." Theo was broken by the loss, and six months later, almost to the day, followed his brother. They rest side by side in a small churchyard at Auvers.

Is there someone in your life whom you have been meaning to write, tomorrow or next week, a letter of friendship, appreciation, congratulations, or condolence? Why not write that letter today? In the process, you will exercise your verbal muscles and lift the spirits of the lucky recipient. As William Swanson observes, "A good letter, in the era of communications satellites and quipping note paper, is something akin to a hand-made afghan or a jar of homemade currant preserves: a small act of grace, a hand-wrought gift from one human being to another." Letters are gifts that take time to make, the kind of time that means you care. You invest only the cost of a stamp—and the gracious impulse to open your heart and mind and communicate with a fellow rider on our planet.

V

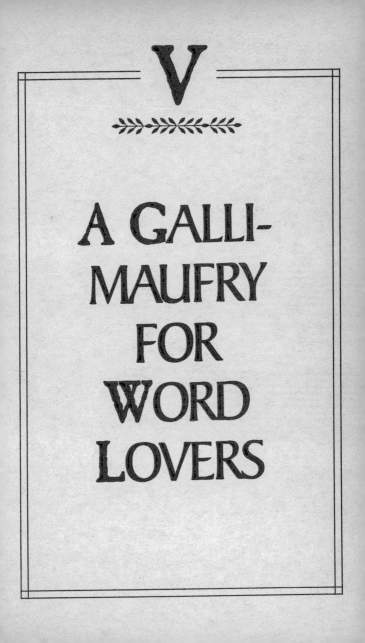

A GALLI-MAUFRY FOR WORD LOVERS

WORDS ABOUT
WORDS

"**G**ive me a lever long enough and a prop strong enough," wrote Archimedes, "and I can single-handed move the world." Riposted Joseph Conrad more than two thousand years later, "Do not talk to me of Archimedes' lever. He was an absent-minded person with a mathematical imagination. Give me the right word and the right accent, and I will move the world."

A persuasive testimonial to the miracle of language is that, for at least three millennia, so many people have talked and written about it. Innumerable men and women, whether serious students of language or not, have turned phrases about language, praising its power or bewailing its abuse, genuflecting to its glory or tweaking its peculiarities.

Thinkers about language don't always agree. "O wondrous power of words!" exults William Wordsworth. "Fine words butter no parsnips," observes an English proverb with less enthusiasm. "How long a time lies in one little word!" Shakespeare rejoices. "Words mean one thing on Monday and another on Tuesday," counters Franklin P. Adams. "Language, I think, belongs to two groups only: gifted individuals everywhere, who use it imaginatively; and the fellowship of men and women, wherever they are, who, without being particularly inventive, nevertheless endeavor to speak and write correctly. Language, however, does not belong to the illiterate or to bodies of people forming tendentious and propagandistic interest groups, determined to use it for what they (usually mistakenly) believe to be their advantage," thunders John Simon. "Language is not an abstract construction of the learned or of dictionary makers, but something arising out of the work, needs, joys, tears, affections, tastes of long generations of humanity and has its bases broad and low, close to the ground," shouts back Walt Whitman with a barbaric yawp.

That statements about words can contradict each other is proof of the ability of language to express a variety of opinions. Quotations disagree even about quotations: "A short saying oft contains wisdom," proclaims Sophocles. "I hate quotations. Tell me what you know," replies Ralph Waldo Emerson (who is quoted twice in this chapter). Ultimately, I side with Benjamin Disraeli's judgment in the matter: "Those who never quote, in return are never quoted." Or maybe George Bernard Shaw had the right idea: "I often quote myself. It adds spice to my conversation."

May the following words about words butter your parsnips and add spice to your conversation and your writing:

By words the mind is excited and the spirit elated.

ARISTOPHANES

A man's command of the language is most important. Next to kissing, it's the most exciting form of communication mankind has evolved.

OREN ARNOLD

A word after a word after a word is power.

MARGARET ATWOOD

I cannot speak well enough to be unintelligible.

JANE AUSTEN

The ill and unfitting choice of words wonderfully obstructs the understanding.

FRANCIS BACON

The root function of language is to control the universe by describing it.

JAMES BALDWIN

Words may be made to disgorge the past that is bottled up inside of them, as coal and wine when we kindle or drink them yield up their bottled sunshine.

OWEN BARFIELD

Language, like the weather, is a popular topic: everybody's got something to say about it. And like the weather, where there is language, there is also change.

DENNIS BARON

"Plain English"—everybody loves it, demands it—from the other fellow.

JACQUES BARZUN

All words are pegs to hang ideas on.

HENRY WARD BEECHER

We need new words—and great ones—to match the present, to build for the future that must be.

STEPHEN VINCENT BENÉT

The turn of a sentence has decided the fate of many a friendship and, for aught we know, the fate of many a kingdom.

JEREMY BENTHAM

A civilization which loses its power over its own language has lost its power over the instrument by which it thinks.

HENRY BESTON

It is the word which opens the door of the treasure cave, the word which builds the universe and commands its power.

G. H. BONNER

Sir Joshua Reynolds once asked Dr. Johnson by what means he had attained his extraordinary accuracy and flow of language. He told him that he had early laid it down as a fixed rule to do his best on every occasion, and in every company; to impart whatever he knew in the most forcible language he could put it in; and that by constant practice and never suffering any careless expressions to escape him or attempting to deliver his thoughts without arranging them in the clearest manner, it became habitual to him.

JAMES BOSWELL

Words, I think, are the one great exhaustless charm and resource of life; and to think how people fling them about and stab and sting and poison, and go their way and forget.

GAMALIEL BRADFORD

Words are as vital to life as food and drink and sex, but on the whole we don't show as much interest in language as we do in the other—more obvious—pleasures.

GYLES BRANDRETH

Words are as recalcitrant as circus animals, and the unskilled trainer can crack his whip at them in vain.

GERALD BRENAN

Great leaders are great leaders because through their command of vocabulary power and culture, they are able to make others see and feel what they see and feel. Gain this power for yourself and you will have at your service the greatest force ever put into the hands of mankind.

JOSEPH G. BRIN

Standard English is a convenient abstraction, like the average man.

G. L. BROOK

To be a collector of language is an innocent occupation. The snatchers and hoarders of birds' eggs and of flowers first create a scarcity, then hunt down the rarities (or, even worse, hire others to go marauding for them), and finally exterminate the beauty which they crave. . . . To hunt words is to do no trespass.

IVOR BROWN

So many people use language as a mere waste product that we may be experiencing a social revolution simply through loss of meanings. If an idea or feeling falls out of our vocabulary, it will probably disappear from our lives.

ANATOLE BROYARD

The magic of the tongue is the most dangerous of all spells.

EDWARD BULWER-LYTTON

A very great part of the mischiefs in this world arises from words.

EDMUND BURKE

Words are like planets, each with its own gravitational pull.

KENNETH BURKE

Oaths are but words and words are but wind.

SAMUEL BUTLER

Words are things; and a small drop of ink,
Falling like dew upon a thought, produces
That which makes thousands, perhaps millions,
    think.

LORD BYRON

An unusual word should be shunned as a ship would shun a reef.

JULIUS CAESAR

There is no material with which human beings work which has so much potential energy as words.

ERNEST ELMO CALKINS

The coldest word was once a glowing new metaphor.

THOMAS CARLYLE

You know that even forms of speech can change
Within a thousand years, and words we know
Were useful once, seem to us wondrous strange
Foolish or forced—and yet men spoke them so.

GEOFFREY CHAUCER

Seek always for the best words and the happiest expression you can find.

LORD CHESTERFIELD

The manner of your speaking is full as important as the matter, as more people have ears to be tickled than understanding to judge.

LORD CHESTERFIELD

Tell me how much a nation knows about its own language, and I will tell you how much that nation knows about its own identity.

JOHN CIARDI

You have to fall in love with hanging around words.

JOHN CIARDI

Words . . . are a kind of natural resource; it is impossible to have too many of them.

ROBERT CLAIBORNE

Language is the armory of the human mind; and at once contains the trophies of its past, and the weapons of its future conquests.

SAMUEL TAYLOR COLERIDGE

Let your speech be always with grace, seasoned with salt, that ye may know how ye ought to answer every man.

COLOSSIANS

Without knowing the force of words it is impossible to know men.

CONFUCIUS

The whole end of speech is to be understood.

CONFUCIUS

If language is not correct, then what is said is not what is meant; if what is said is not what is meant, then what must be done remains undone; if this remains undone, morals and art will deteriorate; if justice goes astray, the people will stand about in helpless confusion. Hence there must be no arbitrariness in what is said. This matters above everything.

CONFUCIUS

Giving the English language to the Americans is like giving sex to small children. They know it's important, but they don't know what to do with it.

MORTON COOPER

Except ye utter by the tongue words easy to be understood, how shall it be known what is spoken? For ye shall speak unto the air.

I CORINTHIANS

In language, as in mathematics, the shortest distance between two points is a straight line.

LOIS DE BAKEY

As a vessel is known by its sound, whether it be cracked or not, men are proved by their speeches whether they be wise or foolish.

DEMOSTHENES

A word in earnest is as good as a speech.

CHARLES DICKENS

A word is dead
When it is said,
Some say.
I say it just
Begins to live
That day.

EMILY DICKINSON

Let us deport—with skill—
Let us discourse—with care—
Power exists in Charcoal—
Before it exists in Fire.

EMILY DICKINSON

Man ever had, and ever will have, leave
To coin new words well suited to the age.
Words are like leaves, some wither every year
And every year a younger race succeeds.

WENTWORTH DILLON

Words are absolutely necessary for thinking, and with a minimum of words there is a minimum of thought.

AUBREY A. DOUGLAS

In particular, one may protest the misuse of our language by those who should know better: businessmen, educators, holders of high offices, and representatives of the news media. If happy illiterates can enrich a language, the pompous half-educated only succeed in impoverishing it.

PHILIP DUNNE

Words are the legs of the mind; they bear it about, carry it from point to point, bed it down at night, and keep it off the ground and out of the marsh and mists.

RICHARD EDER

. . . Words strain,
Crack and sometimes break under the burden,
Under the tension, slip, slide, perish,
Decay with imprecision, will not stay in place
Will not stay still.

T. S. ELIOT

Language is a city to the building of which every human being brought a stone.

RALPH WALDO EMERSON

Every word was once a poem.

RALPH WALDO EMERSON

Words and feathers are tossed by the wind.

ENGLISH PROVERB

A word fitly spoken is like apples of gold in a setting of silver.

ENGLISH PROVERB

A man of words and not deeds is like a garden full of weeds.

ENGLISH PROVERB

Treat words as a Victorian gentleman treated a lady: as his superior, certainly, but never his equal. Cosset them. Defer to them. Tell them how beautiful they are. Give them your seat in the subway. But don't let them break your heart as I have let them break mine.

WILLARD R. ESPY

Words are the tools for the job of saying what you want to say. And what you want to say are your thoughts and feelings, your desires and your dislikes, your hopes and your fears, your business and your pleasure—almost everything, indeed, that makes up you. Except for our vegetablelike growth and our animallike impulses, almost all that we are is related to our use of words. Man has been defined as a tool-using animal, but his most important tool, the one that distinguishes him from all other animals, is his speech.

BERGAN EVANS

The English language has far more lives than a cat. People have been murdering it for years.

FARMERS' ALMANAC

The word makes men free. Whoever cannot express himself is a slave. Speaking is an act of freedom; the word is freedom itself.

LUDWIG FEUERBACH

A favorite proverb of the picture-and-diagram lovers is "One picture is worth more than a thousand words." It simply isn't so. Try to teach people with a picture and you may find that you need a thousand words to tell them exactly what to look at and why.

RUDOLF FLESCH

Good words anoint a man; ill words kill a man.

FLORIO

How do I know what I think until I see what I say?

E. M. FORSTER

All the fun's in how you say a thing.

ROBERT FROST

Half the world is composed of people who have something to say and can't, and the other half who have nothing to say and keep on saying it.

ROBERT FROST

Soft words are hard arguments.

THOMAS FULLER

When words fail, wars begin. When wars finally end, we settle our disputes with words.

WILFRED FUNK

The highest cultural achievement of any nation, the arts notwithstanding, is its language.

EDWARD G. and RICHARD S. GANNON

We fall upon a cliché as if it were a sofa not a sword; for we have rehearsed "good morning" and "how are you?" and "have a nice day" to the place where the tongue is like a stale bun in the mouth.

WILLIAM GASS

There is nothing so hard to kill as a word.

ARTHUR GILMAN

A language owes most of its vigor not to what it rejects but to what it can incorporate within itself.

JOHANN VON GOETHE

Everyone hears only what he understands.

JOHANN VON GOETHE

Every word we know makes a difference, because every word is an idea.

ROBERT GREENMAN

Language is fossil poetry which is constantly being worked over for the uses of speech. Our commonest words are worn-out metaphors.

JAMES BRADSTREET GREENOUGH
and GEORGE LYMAN KITTREDGE

It is obvious that we cannot begin to be citizens in a democracy if we are only partly capable of understanding our own language, if we cannot distinguish critically between truth and falsehood, between sense and nonsense, if we do not realize that language and the word are still more powerful than the atom bomb, that like a weapon it can be used for or against us.

VICTOR GROVE

Words—so innocent and powerless as they are, standing in a dictionary, how potent for good and evil they become, in the hands of one who knows how to combine them!

NATHANIEL HAWTHORNE

Words are the only things that last forever; they are more durable than the eternal hills.

WILLIAM HAZLITT

As men abound in copiousness of language, so

they become more wise, and more mad than ordinary.

THOMAS HOBBES

Life and language are alike sacred. Homicide and verbicide—that is, violent treatment of a word with fatal results to its legitimate meaning—are alike forbidden.

OLIVER WENDELL HOLMES, SR.

When I feel inclined to read poetry, I take down my dictionary. The poetry of words is quite as beautiful as the poetry of sentences.

OLIVER WENDELL HOLMES, SR.

A word is not a crystal, transparent and unchanging. It is the skin of living thought.

OLIVER WENDELL HOLMES, JR.

The self is surrounded by mirrors of language.

HANS HORMANN

Words are the soul's ambassadors, who go Abroad upon her errands to and fro.

JAMES HOWELL

Thanks to words, we have been able to rise above the brutes; and thanks to words, we have often sunk to the level of demons.

ALDOUS HUXLEY

The most valuable of all talents is that of never using two words when one will do.

THOMAS JEFFERSON

Every time a man opens his mouth he says considerably more than he utters.

GARY JENNINGS

In his whole life man achieves nothing so great and so wonderful as what he achieved when he learned to talk.

OTTO JESPERSEN

In the beginning was the Word; and the Word was with God; and the Word was God.

THE GOSPEL ACCORDING TO JOHN

How forcible are right words.

THE GOSPEL ACCORDING TO JOHN

It is not only true that the language we use puts words in our mouths; it also puts notions in our heads.

WENDELL JOHNSON

Language most shows a man; speak that I may see thee.

BEN JONSON

Words, like eyeglasses, obscure everything they do not make clear.

JOSEPH JOUBERT

Before using a fine word, make a place for it.

JOSEPH JOUBERT

Like the fabled Jabberwock, words have jaws that bite and claws that catch.

JAMES J. KILPATRICK

We see words that blow like leaves in the winds of autumn—golden words, bronze words, words that catch the light like opals. We learn that words have an independent life of their own, grown out of echoes and connotations and associations. We see that words are tactile; we find rough words, smooth words, words with splintered edges, words to shout or whisper with, words that caress, words that strike.

JAMES J. KILPATRICK

Words are, of course, the most powerful drug used by mankind.

RUDYARD KIPLING

Without language, it is safe to say that man would not have become fully human.

WESTON LABARRE

True eloquence consists of saying all that should be, not all that could be, said.

LA ROCHEFOUCAULD

Language plays a tremendous role in human affairs. It serves as a means of cooperation and as a weapon of conflict. With it, men can solve problems, erect the towering structures of science and poetry—and talk themselves into insanity and social confusion.

IRVING J. LEE

All I can say is that even if language is a living, evolving organism, it doesn't mean we have to embrace all the changes that occur during our lifetimes. Anyway, if language is so alive, it stands to reason it can get sick.

CHRISTOPHER LEHMANN-HAUPT

If the art of conversation stood a little bit higher, we would have a lower birthrate.

STANISLAW LEM

Our language, one of our most precious natural resources, is also a dwindling one that deserves at least as much protection as our woodlands, streams, and whooping cranes.

JAMES LIPTON

So difficult is it to show the various meanings and imperfections of words when we have nothing else but words to do it with.

JOHN LOCKE

Language is an inventory of human experience.

L. W. LOCKHART

Axes and atom bombs can change the material world, but only language can alter human ideas.

H. C. LONQUET-HIGGINS

No one who has once taken the language under his care can ever again be really happy.

THOMAS LOUNSBURY

It is fatal to the highest success to have command of a noble language and have nothing to say in it; it is equally fatal to have noble thoughts and to lack the power of giving them expression.

HAMILTON WRIGHT MABIE

Change is legitimate and inevitable, for our language is a mighty river, picking up silt and flotsam here and discarding it there, but growing ever wider and richer.

ROBERT MACNEIL

Speech is civilization itself. The word, even the most contradictory word, preserves contact. It is silence which isolates.

THOMAS MANN

When baffled lips demanded speech,
Speech trembled into birth—
One day the lyric word shall reach
From earth to laughing earth.

DON MARQUIS

Language is . . . the beginning of responsibility, a word whose Latin root means to respond (answer, justify, defend). Without language we can react like the beasts and the fishes; with it we can respond like men and women, responsibly. One of the things we are responsible for is language itself, next to life our most precious possession.

WILLIAM MCPHERSON

A living language is like a man suffering incessantly from small hemorrhages, and what it needs above all else is constant transactions of new blood from other tongues. The day the gates go up, that day it begins to die.

H. L. MENCKEN

Language is a growing thing that, like a corn crop, has many uses. As a staple, corn feeds people, horses, and hogs; language also serves utilitarian ends. As a colorless liquid, corn intoxicates. So does language, fermented in a sermon, distilled in a song or story. Corn was made for people, not the other way around. So too with language.

JIM WAYNE MILLER

His words, like so many nimble servitors, trip about him at command.

JOHN MILTON

By winning words to conquer willing hearts
And make persuasion do the work of Fear.

JOHN MILTON

Destroy language and, with it, all things and concepts. The rest is silence.

CHRISTIAN MORGENSTERN

Words are a commodity in which there is never any slump.

CHRISTOPHER MORLEY

Without words man lives his span of years and dies like any other animal; but with language he can make a record of his past and preserve the knowledge and ideas that can help him plan his future and become part of history, rather than remain a mere speck in an ever-shifting present.

ROBERT E. MORSBERGER

Language, like the body, is so comfortable and familiar that we hardly notice its presence or its complexity. Yet once examined closely, the accomplishment of any ordinary speaker is rather astonishing.

RICHARD OHMANN

To degrade language is to degrade civilization.

ERIC PARTRIDGE

If you scoff at language study, how, save in terms of language, will you scoff?

MARIO PEI

When the mind is thinking, it is talking to itself.

PLATO

True wit is Nature to advantage dressed,
What oft was thought, but ne'er so well expressed.

ALEXANDER POPE

Words are like leaves; and where they most
    abound,
Much fruit of sense beneath is rarely found.

ALEXANDER POPE

A good word makes the heart glad.

PROVERBS

His words were softer than oil, yet were they
drawn swords.

PSALMS

If your language is confused, your intellect, if
not your whole character, will almost certainly
correspond.

ARTHUR QUILLER-COUCH

One should not aim at being possible to understand, but at being impossible to misunderstand.

QUINTILLIAN

God . . . has impressed man with no characteristic so proven to distinguish him from the other animals, as by the faculty of speech.

QUINTILLIAN

He that uses many words for explaining any subject doth, like the cuttlefish, hide himself for the most part in his own ink.

JOHN RAY

The grossest thing in our gross national product today is our language. It is suffering from inflation.

JAMES RESTON

Words, like flowers, have their colours too.

ERNEST RHYS

. . . A word has its use,
Or, like a man, it will soon have a grave.

EDWIN ARLINGTON ROBINSON

Time had no special significance for a certain juvenile and incorrigible fisher of words who thought nothing of fishing for two weeks to catch a stanza, or even a line, that he would not throw back into a squirming sea of language where there was every word but the one he wanted. There were strange and iridescent and impossible words that would seize the bait and swallow the hook and all but drag the excited angler in after them, but like that famous catch of Hiawatha's, they were generally not the fish he wanted. He wanted fish that were smooth and shining and subtle, and very much alive, and not too strange, and presently, after long patience and many rejections, they began to bite.

EDWIN ARLINGTON ROBINSON

Scarcely any of our intellectual operations could be carried on to any considerable extent without the agency of words.

PETER ROGET

With words alone, you don't make the soup.

ROMANIAN PROVERB

Words are not our tools; since Adam first called things good and evil, men have cried, spoken, shrieked, screamed, sung, called, and commanded because they must, not because they would. True language is an expression of necessity, not a tool in man's hand.

EUGEN ROSENSTOCK-HUESSEY

No matter how eloquently a dog may bark, he cannot tell you that his parents were poor but honest.

BERTRAND RUSSELL

Names are the definition which we give to the indefinable.

GEORGE RYLANDS

If . . . you are willing to think about how we communicate, and consider the words and the forms of grammar, then you are automatically a member of the Authority, entitled to a ring and a secret handshake and the thrill of membership. A word of warning: If you get hooked on the study of the language, you are in that sorority, or fraternity, for life.

WILLIAM SAFIRE

A mania for neatness drains the blood from the grinning cheeks of language.

WILLIAM SAFIRE

Every utterance is an event, and no two events are precisely alike. The extreme view, therefore, is that no word ever means the same thing twice.

LOUIS B. SALOMAN

Most people have to talk so that they won't hear.

MAY SARTON

Syllables govern the world.

JOHN SELDEN

The manner of saying or doing anything goes a great way in determining the value of the thing itself.

SENECA

Mend your speech a little,
Lest it may mar your fortunes.

WILLIAM SHAKESPEARE

My words fly up, my thoughts remain below:
Words without thoughts never to heaven go.

WILLIAM SHAKESPEARE

Talkers are no good doers.

WILLIAM SHAKESPEARE

You taught me language, and my only profit on't is that I learn'd how to curse.

WILLIAM SHAKESPEARE

Words, words, words.

WILLIAM SHAKESPEARE

Remember that you are a human being with a soul and the divine gift of articulate speech; that your native tongue is the language of Shakespeare and Milton and the Bible; and don't sit there crooning like a bilious pigeon.

GEORGE BERNARD SHAW

Language is a perpetual Orphic song.

PERCY BYSSHE SHELLEY

Words too are known by the company they keep.

JOSEPH SHIPLEY

When it comes to learning good English, most people are prone to be supine.

JOHN SIMON

Like a rat-catcher, a word-catcher has worked hard to master the secrets of his trade.

JAMES SLEDD

Language is the memory of the human race.

WILLIAM HENRY SMITH

It is with words as with sunbeams. The more they are condensed, the deeper they burn.

ROBERT SOUTHEY

The language is no longer lived; it is merely spoken.

GEORGE STEINER

Man does not live by words alone, despite the fact that sometimes he has to eat them.

ADLAI STEVENSON

Perhaps of all the creations of man language is the most astonishing.

LYTTON STRACHEY

I find vocabulary to be a great drawback.

ELIZABETH TAYLOR

A word to the wise is sufficient.

TERENCE

One always refers to language as a tool; but after playing around with more years than there legitimately are, I tell you that it is also, in a vulgar phrase, *something else.* More precious than pearls at any price, it is a marvelous toy, a plaything of the mind.

JOE D. THOMAS

A living language is an expanding language, to be sure, but care should be taken itself that the language does not crack like a dry stick in the process, leaving us all miserably muddled in a monstrous miasma of mindless and meaningless mumbling.

JAMES THURBER

Words cannot control us unless we desire to be controlled by them.

LIONEL TRILLING

English is a language of marvelous qualities. I like to see it properly used just as one likes to see a shirt properly washed and a dinner table properly set.

BARBARA TUCHMAN

If you can teach me a new word, I'll walk all the way to China to get it.

TURKISH PROVERB

First, verily, are words produced, and the mind runs after them.

VEDIC COMMENTARY

I have always suspected that correctness is the last refuge of those who have nothing to say.

FRIEDRICH WASIMAN

Words should be an intense pleasure, just as leather should be to a shoemaker.

EVELYN WAUGH

If all my possessions were to be taken from me with one exception, I would choose to keep the power of communication, for by it I would regain all the others.

DANIEL WEBSTER

Language, as well as the faculty of speech, was the immediate gift of God.

NOAH WEBSTER

Stability in language is synonymous with rigor mortis.

ERNEST WEEKLEY

A language is a dialect that has an army and navy.

MAX WEINREICH

A new word is like a wild animal you have caught. You must learn its ways and break it before you can use it.

H. G. WELLS

The crudest savage may unconsciously manipulate with effortless ease a linguistic system so intricate, manifoldly systematized, and intellectually difficult, that it requires the lifetime study of our greatest scholars to describe its workings.

BENJAMIN LEE WHORF

Uttering a word is like striking a note on the keyboard of the imagination.

LUDWIG WITTGENSTEIN

A SECULAR THANKS-GIVING

We give thanks for language—the human essence, the skin of thought, more to the mind than light is to the eye.

May we try not only to talk, but to say something; not only to hear, but to listen; not only to write, but to communicate.

May our thoughts and aspirations become words that serve to build bridges from mind to mind and from heart to heart, creating a fellowship of those who would hold fast to that which is good.

INDEX

Académie Française, 19, 31, 32, 104
Adages, 78
Adams, Franklin P., 206
Addison, Joseph, 164
Ade, George, 90
Adventures of Huckleberry Finn, The (Clemens), 123, 124–25, 126, 198–99
Adventures of Tom Sawyer, The (Clemens), 124
Advertising
  redundancy in, 74–75
Aiken, Robert, 114
Alexandrov, Vladimir, 178
Alice's Adventures in Wonderland (Dodgson), 116, 117–18, 119, 195
All My Pretty Ones (Sexton), 99
All Our Yesterdays (Robinson), 100
Allen, Fred, 113
All's Well That Ends Well, (Shakespeare), 101
Alton, Louis D', 100
American English, 31–32, 47
  Clemens and, 125–27
  new words in (1980s), 44–48
  Orwell's contribution to, 153
American Language, The (Mencken), 65

American literature
  influence of Clemens on, 125–27
American writing
  quotations from T. S. Eliot on, 142–45
Anagrams, 92, 117
Anderson, Maxwell, 100
Angles (tribe), 21
Anglo-French language, 77–78
Anglo-Saxon language, 21, 22, 23, 25
Angoff, Martin, 178
Antony and Cleopatra (Shakespeare), 101
Archimedes, 205
Arlen, Michael, 27
Arnold, Matthew, 179
As You Like It (Shakespeare), 101
At Heaven's Gate (Warren), 101
Atomic bomb, 83
Auchincloss, Louis, 100
Auden, W. H., 101, 165

Bacon, Francis, 90, 162
Baker, Stephen, 27–28
Bancroft, Lord, 113
Bare Ruined Choirs (Wills), 101
Barren Ground (Glasgow), 100
Barrie, James, 100

Barry, Philip, 100
"Because I Could Not Stop for Death" (Dickinson), 139
Behrans, David, 69
Behrmann, S. N., 100
Bell, Book, and Candle (Druten), 101
Bellafiore, Joseph, 25
Berle, Milton, 113
Berlitz, Charles, 20
Bertram, James, 91
Bettencourt, Michael, 179
Bierce, Albert, 109
Bierce, Ambrose, 108–14
Birkner, Michael, 172
Black (word), 53–55
Blacks, 53–55
Blair, Eric Arthur. *See* Orwell, George (pseud. of Eric Blair)
Bly, Robert, 179
Boleyn, Anne, 141
Bolger, William F., 194
Book of Prefaces, A (Mencken), 6
Bookmobiles, 161
Books, 159–67
Boorstin, Daniel J., 172
Boston Globe, 153
Boswell, James, 102
Both Your Houses (Anderson), 100
Bradbury, Ray, 99
Brander, Laurence, 150, 152–53
Brave New World (Huxley), 100
Brilliant, Ashleigh, 167
Britannia, 21
British Broadcasting Corporation (BBC), 30–31, 147, 150
Brodsky, Joseph, 179
Brotherton, Alice, 163
Browne, Sir Thomas, 90
Browning, Robert, 90
Broyard, Anatole, 160
Brudnell, James Thomas, Earl of Cardigan, 82
Bulwer-Lytton, Edward, 160
Burgess, Anthony, 101
Burgess, Gelett, 90
Burke, Edmund, 162
Business
  new words in, 45–46
Butler, Samuel, 165
Byron, George Gordon, 90

Caen, Herb, 69
Caesar, Gaius Julius, 22
Cakes and Ale (Maugham), 100
Calvino, Italo, 162
Cane, Melville, 139–40
Canterbury Tales, The (Chaucer), 60, 125
Capek, Karel, 91
Captain Kangaroo, 194
Carlyle, Thomas, 90, 163
Carroll, Lewis. *See* Dodgson, Charles Lutwidge (Lewis Carroll)
Carter, James Stewart, 100
Castro, Fidel, 31
Catch-22 (Heller), 88–89
Cather, Willa, 90
Cats (musical), 142
Cawdray, Robert, 102–03
"Charge of the Light Brigade, The" (Tennyson), 81–82
Charlemagne, king of France, 21
Chaucer, Geoffrey, 60, 88, 125
Cheever, John, 171
Chesterfield, Lord, 90
China, 80
Chinese language, 20, 78, 80
Chomsky, Noam, 17–18
Christie, Agatha, 99
Chronicles of Wasted Time (Muggeridge), 101
Churchill, Winston, 34, 82, 112, 165
Ciardi, John, 179
Cibber, Colley, 90
Cicero, 163
Clemens, Samuel Langhorne (Mark Twain), xiv–xv, 90, 123–34, 198–99
  views on style and language, 127–31
Clichés, 129
Coca-Cola, 80
Cocteau, Jean, 179
Coleridge, Samuel Taylor, 90
Communication failures, 82–83
Concord, Mass., Public Library Committee, 198–99
Conciseness, 128–29, 185
Congreve, William, 178
Conrad, Joseph, 205
Couplets, 187, 190–91

Coutts, Henry T., 165
covivant, 70–71
Coward, Noel, 101
Crimean War, 81–82
Cry Havoc (Sadler), 100
Cuba, 31
Cuisine
  new words in, 47
Culture
  and language, 51
Cymbeline (Shakespeare), 101

Dahl, Roald, xx
Daiches, David, 162
Danes, 22
Daniel, Samuel, 19, 23, 24
Dark Ages, 21
Davis, Ossie, 53
Dawsoh, George, 172
Day, Mollie, 109
Dear Brutus (Barrie), 100
"Death of the Hired Man" (Frost), 35
Denmark, 20
Descartes, René, 165
Devil's Dictionary, The (Bierce), 108, 110–12
De Voto, Bernard, 162
Dialect, 125, 127
Dick, Philip K., 100
Dickinson, Emily, 134–40, 161, 179, 182
Dickson, Paul, 171
Dictionaries, 93, 102–8, 114, 131
Dictionary of the English Language (Johnson), 102–08
Disney, Walt, 164
Disraeli, Benjamin, 206
Dodgson, Charles Lutwidge (Lewis Carroll), 90, 115–22
  letter writing, 195–96
Dogs of War, The (Stone), 100
Dorgan, T. A., 90
Doublespeak, 154–56
Doublets (game), 120, 122
Downey, Mike, 144–45
Dryden, John, 90
Duckworth, Rev. Robinson, 115–16
Dumas, Alexandre, 95
Dunne, Finley Peter, 90
Dutch language, 78

Dyer's Hand, The (Auden), 101

Editorial *we*, 129
Egbert, king of Englaland, 21
Eliot, Andrew, 141–42
Eliot, Charles, 165
Eliot, Thomas Stearns, 141–45, 186
Elyot, Sir Thomas, 89, 141
Emerson, Ralph Waldo, 26, 206
Englaland, 21
England, 22, 24
English grammar, 11–16, 130
  simplicity of, 24, 27, 28
English language, 19–32
  borrowed words in, 22–23, 25–26, 29
  brevity, conciseness of, 28–29
  ease of learning, 26, 27–28
  flaws in, 51
  as global language, 19, 20–21, 24, 29–32
  history of, xv, 21–24, 60
  influence of Shakespeare on, 94–97
  Orwell on, 148–49
  playfulness of, 38–43
  prejudice in, 51–61
  see also American English
"English Uber Alles" (Lowenstern), 30
Entertainment
  new words in, 47
Epsom, N. H., 64–65
Epstein, Joseph, 164
Erasmus, Desiderius, 161
Essayists, 88
Euclid and His Modern Rivals (Dodgson), 119
Evans, Malcolm, 100
Evil That Men Do, The (Hill), 100

Fadiman, Clifton, 109, 162
Faerie Queene, The (Spenser), 88
Faulkner, William, 99
Ferguson, Francis, 101
"Figure a Poem Makes, The" (Frost), 183
Foot (feet) (poetry), 189–91
Foote, Samuel, 90
Ford, Ford Madox, 100

Fortune and Men's Eyes (Herbert), 101
Fortune's Fool (Reynolds), 100
France, Anatole, 167
Frank, Anne, 7–9
Free verse, 187–89
Freeman, B. Freer, 67
French language, xv, 20, 21, 24, 27, 77
    American words in, 31–32
    influence on English, 21–22, 23, 25
    vocabulary, 24
Frost, Robert, 35, 99, 135, 179, 183
Fry, Christopher, 179
Full Fathom Five (Carter), 100
funny bone, 41

Garrick, David, 104
Gender bias. *See* Sexism
General Motors, 80
German language, 20, 24, 30
Ghostbusters (film), 44
Giant's Strength, A (Sinclair), 101
Gibson, William, 4
Gilfillan, 180
Glasgow, Ellen, 100
Glimpses of the Moon, The (Wharton), 100
Gogh, Theo Van, 199–201
Gogh, Vincent Van, 199–201
Goldsmith, Oliver, 90
Gone With the Wind (Mitchell), 160–61
Gorham High School Library, 173–76
Grasso, Ella, 56
Graves, Robert, 180
"Great Automatic Grammatisator, The" (Dahl), 11
Greek language, 68, 73, 77–78
    influence on English, 22–23, 25
Greene, A. C., 172
Grenada, 156
Grimm, Jakob, 28
Gunther, John, 100

Haiku, 184–86
Halberstam, David, 100
Hall, H., 100
Hall, Rich, 62

Halley's Comet, 123, 132–33
Hamlet (Shakespeare), 95–96, 100
Hardwick, Elizabeth, 166
Harold, king of England, 22
Harris, Jean, 142–43
Hauser, Ernest O., 166
Hawthorne, Nathaniel, 125
Hayakawa, S. I., 166
Hayes, Helen, 171
Hebert, Ernest, 100
Heller, Joseph, 88–89
Hemingway, Ernest, 125, 163
Henry, O., (William Sidney Porter), 90
Henry VIII (Shakespeare), 101
Henry VIII, king of England, 141
Her Privates, We (Manning), 100
Herbert, John, 101
Herrick, Robert, 101
Highet, Gilbert, 164
Hill, R. Lance, 100
"Hill Street Blues" (television program), 144
Hindustani, 20
Hiroshima, 83
Holland, 20
"Hollow Men, The" (Eliot), 145
Homer, 93
Homophones, 41–43
Horwitz, Elinor Lander, 168
Housman, A. E., 178
How Like an Angel (MacDonnell), 100
Howells, William Dean, 124, 132
How Like a God (Stout), 100
Hugo, Victor, 171
Humanness
    language as hallmark of, xiv, 3, 17, 243
Humor
    Clemens on, 131
Hunting of the Snark, The (Dodgson), 195
Hurricane names, 60
Huxley, Aldous, 100, 166

"I Felt a Curious Tickle" (Horne), 138
"I Taste a Liquor Never Brewed" (Dickinson), 182
Ides of March, The (Wilder), 100

Imagery, 142, 185–86
In Praise of Folly (Erasmus), 161
India, 20, 30
Indifferent Children, The (Auchin-
closs), 100
Indonesian language, 20
Iraq, 156
Irving, Washington, 90
It Was the Nightingale (Ford), 100
Italian language, 24, 78
Ivanhoe (Scott), xv

"Jabberwocky" (Dodgson), 118–19
James, Henry, 91
James I, king of England, 97
Japan
World War II, 82–83
Japanese language, 20, 31, 78
Jimenez, Ralph, 144
Johnson, Lady Bird, 172
Johnson, Samuel, 90, 102–14, 180
Johnson, William H., 35
Jonson, Ben, 89, 93
Julius Caesar (Shakespeare), 100
Jutes (tribe), 21

Kafka, Franz, 166
Katzenbach, Larry, 177
Keillor, Garrison, 164
Keller, Helen, 4–5, 7, 9, 165
Kellerman, Faye, 100
Kennedy, John F., 180
Kennedy, X. J., 180
Kernan, F. G., 114
Kieran, John, 166
Kilpatrick, James J., 45
King James Bible, 35, 93, 97–99
King John (Shakespeare), 101
King Lear (Shakespeare), 101
Knight, Eric, 100
Kuwait, 156

Lander, 167
Language(s), xiv–xv
Dickinson's use of, 135
Dodgson's attitude toward func-
tion of, 120–22
Eliot's use of, 145
emancipating power of, 4–10

figurative, 186
flaws in, 51
as hallmark of humanness, xiv,
xvi–xvii, 3, 17, 243
invention of, 16–18, 87
Johnson and, 102, 106–08
miracle of, xvi–xvii, 3–10, 205–06
number of, 19–20
of poetry, 182–83
and totalitarianism, 152, 153, 156
see also under specific language,
e.g., English language
Latin language, 22–23, 25, 78
Laurence, Larry, 112
Learning of language, 11–18
Left (word), 52–53
Left-handedness, 52–53, 55
Letter writing, 193–201
Levenson, Sam, 163
Levinson, Leonard, 113
Lewis, Sinclair, 91
Lexicographers, lexicography, 106–
08
Libraries, 5–6, 168–72
quotations about, 171–72
school, 173–76
Liddell, Alice, 116
Liddell, Henry George, 116
Light Thickens (Marsh), 99
Limericks, 191–92
Lincoln, Abraham, 163, 196
Literacy, 7
Literature, 130, 160
see also American literature;
Wordmakers, literary
Little More Than Kin, A (Hebert),
100
Locke, John, 90
London Tribune, 146
Longfellow, Henry Wadsworth, 134,
162
Love (word), 68–69
"Love Song of J. Alfred Prufrock,
The" (Eliot), 143–44, 186
Lover's Meeting (Alton), 100
Love's Labour's Lost (Shakespeare),
95
Lowell, Amy, 166
Lowell, James Russell, 134
Lowenstern, Enno von, 30
Lowes, John Livingston, 97

Macauley, Rose, 99
Macbeth (Shakespeare), 97, 99–100
McDonald, Beverly, 70–71
Mcdonald, Gregory, 100–01
McDonalds, 74
MacDonnell, A. G., 100
McKuen, Rod, 180
MacLean, Allistair, 99
MacLeish, Archibald, 180
Malay language, 78
Malaysia, 20
Malcolm X., 7, 9
Manning, Frederic, 100
Mansfield, Katherine, 166
Marital state
  names and, 59–60
Mark Twain's Autobiography
  (Clemens), 123–24
Marsh, Ngaio, 99
Martins, Joyce, 100
Marx, Groucho, 142
Maugham, W. Somerset, 100, 180
Mayo, William, 114
Measure for Measure (Shakespeare),
  101
Medicine
  new words in, 46–47
Melville, Herman, 90
Mencken, H. L., 6, 65, 91, 114
Merchant of Venice (Shakespeare),
  100
Meredith, William, 192
Merely Players (Mcdonald), 101
Merry Heart, The (Swinnerton), 101
Metaphor, 186–87
Meter, 189–90, 191
Middle Ages, 22
Middle English, xv, 22, 60, 77–78
Middleton, Ellis, 99
Mila 18 (Uris), 89
Miller, Casey, 57–58
Milton, John, 88, 93, 162
Miracle Worker, The (Gibson), 4
Mitchell, Margaret, 160–61
Monroe, Vaughn, 74
Montesquieu, Baron de la Brède et,
  166
Moon Is Down, The (Steinbeck), 100
Moore, Clement Clark, 95
More, Sir Thomas, 89
Morgan, Edward P., 165

Morphemes, 88
Moscow Radio, 30–31
Ms. (term), 59–60
Much Ado About Nothing (Shake-
  speare), 101
Muggeridge, Malcolm, 101
Müller, Max, 3
Murray, Sir James, 107–08
My Mark Twain (Howells), 132

Nabokov, Vladimir, 101
Nagasaki, 83
Naked to Mine Enemies (Ferguson),
  101
Names, naming, 58–59, 62–63
Nash, Ogden, 100
National Christina Foundation, 66–
  67
National Council of Teachers of En-
  glish, Committee on Public
  Doublespeak, 154–55, 156
National Weather Service, 60
Native Tongues (Berlitz), 20
Neologisms
  in literature, 87–91
  in Shakespeare, 93–94
Nevada Territorial Enterprise, 124
New Jersey legislature, 80
New York Times, 30
Newspeak, 151, 153–55
Night Before Christmas, The
  (Moore), 95
Nims, John Frederick, 178
Nineteen Eighty-Four (Orwell),
  146–47, 150–56
Nixon, Richard, 73
No Friendly Drop (Wade), 100
Nobel Prize for literature, 145
Noblest Roman (Halberstam), 100
"Noiseless Patient Spider, A"
  (Whitman), 187–88
Nonsense literature, Clemens on,
  131
Norfolk Prison Colony, 7
Norman Conquest, xv, 21–22
Norman French, 21–22
Normandy, 21
Norris, Al, 65
Norris, Kathleen, 166
Not So Deep as a Well (Parker), 100
Nothing Like the Sun (Burgess), 101

Novelists, 87–88
Number, disagreement of, 58

"Occurrence at Owl Creek Bridge, An" (Bierce), 109
Ode, 191
Of Woman Born (Rich), 99
O'Hara, John, 91
Ohmann, Richard, 16–17
Oke, Richard, 101
Old English, xv, 21
Old Possum's Book of Practical Cats (Eliot), 142
One Touch of Nature (Webster), 101
Orwell, George, 146–56
Othello (Shakespeare), 101
"Out, Out—," (Frost), 99
Overspeak. *See* Redundancy
Oxford English Dictionary, 24, 107, 108

Pakistan, 20
Pale Fire (Nabokov), 101
Paradise Lost (Milton), 88
Parker, Dorothy, 100
Parker, Robert B., 100
Parts of speech, 44
Pasteur Institute of Paris, 32
Pater, Walter, 101
Paul, St., 195
Pepsi-Cola, 79–80
Perchance to Dream (Parker), 100
Perrine, Laurence, 180, 189
Peter, Laurence, 113, 187
Playwrights, 88
Pleonasm(s), 75–78
Poetry writing, 182–92
Poets, poetry, 87–88, 134, 136, 137, 177–81
Political change, 47
Political language, 155
Political overspeak, 73–74
"Politics and the English Language" (Orwell), 147–49, 155
Pomp and Circumstance (Coward), 101
Pope, Alexander 90
Portmanteau words, 118–19
Portuguese language, 20
Positive (the)
  need for words expressing, 66–68

Potsdam Declaration, 82
Potter, Stephen, 91
Pound, Ezra, 91, 180, 186–87
Powers, John, 153
Prejudice in English language, 51–61
Primrose Path, The (Nash), 100
Pronouns, 58, 60, 66
Proust, Marcel, 101
Proverbs, 34
Prufrock, J. Alfred, 143
Puns, 40, 41

Quality of Mercy, The (Kellerman), 100

Racism, 52–55
Radner, Gilda, 79
Rain from Heaven (Behrmann), 100
Ramstrom, Gertrude King, 169–71
Random House Dictionary of the English Language, The, 53–54
Reading
  Clemens on, 131
Reagan, Ronald, 45
Redundancy(ies), 72–78
Remembrance of Things Past (Proust), 101
Renaissance, 22–23
Reynolds, Dorothy, 101
Reynolds, Frederick, 100
Rhyme, 189, 190, 191
Rich, Adrienne, 99
Richard II (Shakespeare), 94
Richard III (Shakespeare), 100
Right (word), 52–53
Robinson, Edward G., 100
Rocco, Mario, 113
Roget's Thesaurus, 27
Romeo and Juliet (Shakespeare), 100
Roosevelt, Franklin D., 160
Rosemary for Remembrance (Martins), 100
Rosenberg, Bernard, 113
Rosencrantz and Guildenstern Are Dead (Stoppard), 100
Rowland, Helen, 113
Rules, internalized, 12, 13, 15
Russian language, 20, 24, 30–31

Sadler, Barry, 100
St. Paul's School, 35–37, 62–63, 72

Salad Days (Reynolds), 101
San Francisco Examiner, 109
San Jose Public Library, 80
Sandburg, Carl, 180
Saturday Night Live (television program), 79
Saxons (tribe), 21, 22
Scarlet Letter, The (Hawthorne), 125
Schnabel, Ernst, 9
Schnitzler, Arthur, 100
Science
  new words in, 46
Scott, Walter, xv
Second-language users of English, 20, 27–28, 30
Seuss, Dr., (Theodore Seuss Geisel), 91
Sexism, 55–61, 66
Sexton, Anne, 99
Shakespeare, William, 34–35, 90, 92–101, 151, 206
  borrowings from, 99–101
  influence on English language, 101
  plays, 92–93, 99–101
  sonnets, 101
Shales, Tom, 144–45
Shaw, George Bernard, 90, 206
Sheridan, Richard Brinsley, 90
Shorer, Mark, 165
Sidney, Sir Philip, 26
Signifying Nothing (Evans), 100
Simon, John, 206
Sinclair, Upton, 101
Six Nations (Native Americans), 197–98
Snark books (Dodgson), 119
Sniglets, 62–63
Social change, 47
Somerset, Fitzroy James Henry, Lord Raglan, 82
Song of Roland, 21
Sonnet(s), 191
  of Shakespeare, 101
Sophocles, 206
Sound and the Fury, The (Faulkner), 99
Soutar, Andrew, 100
Soviet Union, 30, 83
Spanish language, 20, 24, 66
Special Providence, A (Yates), 100

Speech, speaking, 12, 13, 51, 126, 131
Spelling
  Clemens on, 130
Spenser, Edmund, 88
Stalin, Joseph, 82
Stanzas, 191
Steele, Richard, 164
Steinbeck, John, 91, 100
Steinem, Gloria, 55–56, 59
Stern, Judith, 113
Stevenson, Adlai, 73
Stickney, Lorraine, 173
Stone, Robert, 100
Stoppard, Tom, 100
Story of My Life, The (Keller), 5
Stout, Rex, 100
Stowe, Harriet Beecher, 90
Strange Bedfellows (Soutar), 100
Style, 128, 149–50
  of Orwell, 149–50
Sullivan, Anne Mansfield, 4–5
Swanson, William, 201
Sweden, 20
Swift, Jonathan, 90
Swift, Kate, 57–58
Swinnerton, Frank, 101
Switzerland, 20
Synonyms, 26
Syntax, 24

Table Alphabeticall, A (Cawdray), 102–03
Taken at the Flood (Gunther), 100
Tanaguchi Buson, 184–85
Tarnower, Herman, 142
Taylor, Bert, 112
Technology
  and new words, 46, 65–66
Tempest, The (Shakespeare), 93–94, 100
Tennyson, Alfred, 81–82
This Above All (Knight), 100
Thomas, Dylan, 178
Thompson, Dorothy, 26
Thoreau, Henry David, 166, 183
Three Musketeers, The (Dumas), 95
Through the Looking Glass (Dodgson), 116, 120–21, 195
Thurber, James, 154
Tiananmen Square, 156

Time magazine, 142, 143
Time Out of Joint (Dick), 100
Timon of Athens (Shakespeare), 101
Told by an Idiot (Macauley), 99
Tomorrow and Tomorrow (Barry), 100
Translation, 28, 29, 79–80
  error in, 80, 82–83
Trautmann, Les, 162
Troilus and Cressida (Shakespeare), 101
Truman, Harry, 82, 83
Tuchman, Barbara, 163
Turco, Lewis Putnam, 180
Turner, Tina, 68
Twain, Mark. *See* Clemens, Samuel Langhorne (Mark Twain)
Twelfth Night (Shakespeare), 100
Tyndale, William, 89

Uncle Tom's Children (Wright), 6
Undiscovered Country (Schnitzler), 100
United States
  as superpower, 24
U.S. Census Bureau, 70
Untermeyer, 137, 181
Updike, John, 142
Uris, Leon, 89
Usage, 103
Ustinov, Peter, 163

Valiant, The (Hall), 100
Vanity Fair, 120
Vaulting Ambition (Middleton), 99
Vocabulary (English language), 40, 48, 63, 153
  creation of, in literature, 91–97
  fixing, in dictionaries, 106–07
  richness of, 23, 24–29
  in Shakespeare, 93
Voltaire (François Marie Arouet), 163, 181

Wade, Henry, 100
Wagner, Robert, 73
Walpole, Horace, 90
Wanton Boys (Oke), 101
Ward, Artemus, 90
Warren, Robert Penn, 101
Washington Post, 168

"Waste Land, The" (Eliot), 144
Way to Dusty Death, The (MacLean), 99
Web of Life, The (Herrick), 101
Webster, Benjamin, 101
Webster's Third New International Dictionary, 24
Weekley, Ernest, 101
Wharton, Edith, 100
White (word), 54–55
White, E. B., 181
Whitman, Walt, 187–88, 206
Whittier, John Greenleaf, 134
Wilde, Oscar, 95
Wilder, Thornton, 100
William, duke of Normandy, 21–22
William and Mary College, 197–98
Wills, Gary, 101
Winter of Our Discontent (Steinbeck), 100
Wittgenstein, Ludwig, 3, 10
Wolfe, Tom, 45
Women
  stigmatized in English language, 55–61
Woodward, William, 91
Woollcott, Alexander, 116
Word choice
  Clemens on, 127, 128
Word order, 13–15
Word pairs, 75–77
Word play
  in Dodgson, 117–18, 120
Word roots, 77–78
Wordmakers, literary, 87–91
  A. Bierce, 110–12, 114
  S. Clemens, 123–33
  E. Dickinson, 134–40
  C. Dodgson, 115–22
  T. S. Eliot, 141–45
  S. Johnson, 102–10, 114
  G. Orwell, 145–56
  W. Shakespeare, 92–101
Words, 12–13, 18, 23
  abstract, 13
  androgynous, 56
  big, 104–05
  dangers of misunderstanding, 79–83
  inclusive of men and women, 58, 60–61

Words *(cont.)*
  incorporated into other languages, 29–32
  intentionality of, 24
  invention of, 87
  long, 33, 34
  monosyllabic, 34, 35–37
  needed, 62–71
  new, 32, 69–70, 71
    in literature, 87–91
    1980s, 44–48
    in Shakespeare, 93–94
  playful, 40–41
  short, 33–37, 129
  things, ideas and, 62, 63–71
  meaning of, 12–13, 44, 77, 80, 81–82, 153–54

Words and Women (Miller and Swift), 57–58
Wordsworth, William, 181, 205
World War II, 82–83
Wright, Frank Lloyd, 114
Wright, Richard, 5–7, 9
Writing, 51, 193
  American, 142–45
  letters, 193–201
  Orwell's rules of, 149
  poetry, 182–92

Yates, Richard, 100
Yeats, William Butler, 181

Zellerbach, Craig, 113